NOW

BE

HAPPIER

How to Measure Your Happiness Score, Make Changes and Be Happier

Marc Halpern

This book was written and edited entirely by human beings except for two sentences quoted from ChatGPT in Chapter 7 (page 45 in print book).

ISBN 978-1-960953-00-1

Published by Part Time Investors LLC
PO Box 575, Williamstown, New Jersey 08094
www.NowBeHappier.com

I dedicate this book to my parents who emerged from unimaginable tragedy and hardship and instilled in me and in my brother, the highest level of core values, personal ethics, and strong work ethic while serving as outstanding community leaders, mentors and role models in every community in which they lived.

Acknowledgements

I am extremely grateful to my wife for her support and companionship in our 43 years of amazingly stress-free marriage.

I am very proud of my adult children, their wives and our grandchildren, all of whom share the core values and personal ethics being passed down through the generations.

I want to express deep thanks and appreciation to Renen Avneri ("superstar" in my mind) who invested hundreds of hours writing the app **"Be Happier**." Renen is an inspiration to me and all people who apply a positive mindset to be very successful after overcoming significant multiple challenges.

I am very grateful to four close friends who invested their time, intellect and care to critique and improve this book. Thank you to my good friends:

Donna Bauer: https://thenotebuyer.com
Greg Davis: http://GregDsellsRE.com
Ron Odom: https://campostellapropertiesllc.com
Joe Beauchamp

Table of Contents

Preface

If you have common sense, you can change your life and **BE HAPPIER!**

This book will give you very simple, compelling and practical tools to **BE HAPPIER.**

This entire book consists of:

1. One simple formula (that is very easy to understand)
2. A whole lot of common sense

There are no gimmicks in this book. All you need is the desire to **BE HAPPIER**, understand a few simple concepts, like the ones shown in the box below, and be willing to apply common sense when you choose what you do today and every day for the rest of your life.

INVEST Time
Time during which you ENJOY what you are doing without causing harm to yourself or others

SPEND Time
Time during which you DO NOT ENJOY what you are doing but if you didn't do it, it would cause harm

WASTE Time
Time during which you do something that causes HARM to yourself and/or others

SLEEP
Time between when you go to sleep and wake up

You will learn that everything you do fits into one of four categories that are easy to recognize: INVEST time, SPEND time, WASTE time and SLEEP.

In this book, you will learn how to maximize INVEST time which means that you will engage in activities that you enjoy without causing harm.

When you INVEST more of your time, you will experience more joy and fulfillment and you will **BE HAPPIER**. Are you ready to **BE HAPPIER**?

CHAPTER 1
The Goal

The goal of this book is to enable you to **BE HAPPIER**.

If you want to **BE HAPPIER**, proceed to Chapter 2.

CHAPTER 2

What You Must Do

Here is what **this book will do for YOU**:

1. This book will provide you with an extremely simple model to measure your "Happiness Score." The Happiness Score measures your happiness **objectively** on a **continuous basis** with very little effort by you.[1]

2. This book will show you how to identify opportunities to **BE HAPPIER** using an Opportunity Table.[2]

3. This book will provide you with the opportunity to use the Happiness Score and Opportunity Table to make decisions that will enable you to **BE HAPPIER**. Some decisions will be easy and others will be difficult. Some will be daily decisions and others will be once-in-a-lifetime decisions. All of the decisions and actions will be YOURS! Of course, before you make any decision or take any action, you must ensure your safety and well-being.

---

[1] If you download and use the FREE app "**Be Happier**" on your iPhone (Android version will be launched at a later date), the FREE app will continuously calculate and show your Happiness Score. All you will need to do is click on the app 2-8 times per day. The app will not collect your personal information. Only you will have access to your information.

[2] We will show you how to construct your Opportunity Table easily and manually in Chapter 18. While certainly not necessary, you can upgrade the app to conveniently and automatically generate your Opportunity Table on a continuous basis for a nominal fee.

In the end, you and only you are responsible for your happiness, safety and well-being.

Here is what **YOU will do for YOU**:

1. Understand how the simple Happiness Score works.

2. Use the Happiness Score and Opportunity Table to identify opportunities for you to **BE HAPPIER.**

3. Make decisions and take action to **BE HAPPIER.**

Are you ready and willing to **BE HAPPIER**?

If not, don't bother reading this book.

If yes, you are about to embark on a journey filled with a lot of common sense that will result in improving your life!

CHAPTER 3

Why Do We Need a Happiness Score?

In order to design an effective and efficient path to achieve a major goal in life, you need to know where you are now and where you are going.

A GPS app or "map app" provides you with efficient directions to travel from one place to another. In order for a map app to be effective, it must ALWAYS know your current location AND your destination. If you don't know where you are now OR if you don't know where you're going, there is no way that the map app can guide you on the most efficient path (shown by the arrow in the figure).

Fortunately, GPS can figure out where you are, so all you need to know is your destination. Of course, if you don't have a destination, you will wander around aimlessly and never reach your desired destination until and unless you define where you're going.

Similar to a properly working GPS, in order to **BE HAPPIER**, you need to:

1. Know your current happiness level today.

2. Set goals for specific destinations for your happiness level in the future.

3. Design an effective and efficient path to meet your goals.

4. Execute your plan.

You should also add two more steps:

5. Monitor your progress.

6. Reward yourself and celebrate when tangible progress is observed.

Before we tell you how the Happiness Score works in Chapters 4 and 5, please know that there is an iPhone app called "**Be Happier**" (Android app planned for the future) that is free, does not collect any of your personal identifying information and continuously measures your Happiness Score with very little effort on your part (two to eight taps per day depending on how many times you switch from activities you enjoy to activities you don't enjoy). So, if you use the app "**Be Happier**," you will always know "where you are" with your Happiness Score. The app "**Be Happier**" allows you to choose your destination, which is your target Happiness Score and the app helps you monitor your progress along the journey toward your goal.

Once you know your current Happiness Score and your Happiness Score goal, then you can make decisions and take actions to **BE HAPPIER** in an effective and efficient manner. In fact, as you take more control of your life and actions, you will watch your Happiness Score increase.

Increasing your Happiness Score **faster** (i.e., more efficiently) is important in **order to avoid wasting YEARS or DECADES of your life not being happy** (or as happy as you can be).

Let's face it…it's YOUR life and you can control most of your actions that determine your life. But YOU must choose to take control (unless you live in an inescapable dictatorship).

What if you don't know where you are or you don't know where you're going? What happens then? It turns out that most people have no idea where they are or where they're going. They wander around aimlessly without a known destination.

The result…

Most people waste AT LEAST 1-2 decades of their lives, taking the wasteful curved line in the diagram, instead of following the straight line (the shortest distance between two points) while seeking the happiness they want and deserve.

Do you want to take control of your life and **BE HAPPIER** or do you want to waste 1-2 decades of your life (or more!) like most people?

It's your choice.

Really.

CHAPTER 4

What is Happiness?

I suggest that you skip the next paragraph. Do not read the next paragraph.

"Experts" have tried to define happiness and have come up with all kinds of definitions. Scientists have tried to measure happiness in a variety of ways, often winding up with complex questionnaires, that seem to include about 20 questions, then require a large statistically significant set of individuals to self-report *subjective* levels for each answer in order to come up with a correlation that can be used to benchmark the answers of other people who complete the same cumbersome, time-consuming and laborious set of questions and give their own subjective answers that may or may not use the same judgment of the original subjects who completed the questionnaire.

I suggested that you skip the previous paragraph, but most of you read it anyway. I'm glad that you read it anyway. Why? Because you will now appreciate how simple our Happiness Score is when it defines and measures your happiness without complex questionnaires or subjective self-reporting!

I came up with a few common-sense thoughts to define and measure happiness.

Happiness is all about what we do with our time.

I am NOT a psychologist. I have NOT conducted any statistically significant studies of human behavior. I did NOT innovate complex questionnaires. I have no formal credentials for defining happiness…

…except for two absolutely crucial realities:

1. I have achieved a very high level of happiness in relationships, at work and in self-actualization which I analyzed and explain in this book.

2. I have common sense (just like most of you).

The combination of one remarkably simple equation and common sense is the only basis for everything written in this book. Common sense and my track record qualified me to innovate a model for happiness. **Common sense qualifies <u>YOU</u> to judge this model for happiness**.

That means that if you have common sense, you can understand **EVERYTHING** explained here. It also means that you can choose to accept, reject or adapt all or portions of these explanations, as you see fit.

I presented the simple equation and common sense described in this book as a TEDx talk to an audience of high school students in November 2022. The students and teachers asked great questions and appeared to buy into the concepts. I recommend that you watch my 17-minute TEDx talk at https://youtu.be/A9MViB3tS5w.

How simple is the Happiness Score model? It is so simple that you only need 3rd-grade arithmetic to calculate the score. I figured it out in one sitting.

In case you're curious, I came up with this model for happiness on a 15-hour flight from Shanghai to Newark in 2007. I am a research chemist and I had just completed some very good meetings in Asia about phase-transfer catalysis technology (my primary field of expertise). I was feeling pretty good and after watching two movies on the long flight, I still had more than 8 hours left. As the white noise of the airplane droned on and I couldn't fall asleep, I spontaneously decided to figure out why I am happy, what happiness is and how to measure happiness.

I had a lot of data to work with. I was (and still am) very happy with my stress-free decades of marriage with my highly supportive wife since 1980, who enjoyed her own fulfilling job as a teacher. I was (and still am) very happy with the core values of our adult children, one an eagle scout and graduate student at that time and the other a Peace Corps volunteer at the time. I was (and still am) very happy with the thrill of discovery and intellectual stimulation of my work in phase-transfer catalysis since 1976. I was (and still am) happy with my secondary occupation as a part-time real estate investor, which a few years later resulted in financial freedom without driving myself crazy along the journey. I was (and still am) very happy having traveled the world, mostly giving lectures on phase-transfer catalysis in 250 cities at that time (more than 300 today). In fact, I am writing this book in an Airbnb apartment in the Castello district of Venice, that I rented for two weeks to finally document these explanations that I innovated more than 15 years ago on the Shanghai-Newark flight.

In other words, I have an excellent track record in achieving all my goals for happiness in relationships, at work and in self-actualization. Much of my success in my multiple occupations in science and business is a direct result of being able to analyze the key factors for success in any situation, formulate a strategic plan and execute the plan with discipline while making appropriate course corrections to optimize performance.

That is exactly how I approached analyzing the key components of happiness, creating a model for anyone to **BE HAPPIER** and refining the model over 15 years until writing this book and launching the app "**Be Happier**" so that YOU can benefit and improve YOUR life.

I have been the happiest person I know since I got married. I was depressed from childhood until meeting my wife. So, this long plane ride with the seemingly endless white noise was just the right environment to figure out why I was so happy with my life as an adult and why I was not happy earlier in life, especially as a teenager (for example, when I was left back in 11th grade; see the Final Comments chapter at the end of this book).

So, without any preparation or any background information, I had a few hours on a flight to figure out the essence of happiness by just using common sense.

I concluded that **HAPPINESS IS ALL ABOUT WHAT WE DO WITH OUR TIME!**

If we are enjoying what we are doing at a given moment and not causing harm to ourselves, to others or to the environment, that is a good thing.

It makes sense that we would want to maximize the number of such moments from now until the end of our lives.

The concept is simple: **ENJOY WITHOUT CAUSING HARM to yourself or to others**.

Happiness is all about what you do with your time during which you feel joy and fulfillment, in your waking hours from birth until end of life.

> **Goal:**
> **Maximize the time we ENJOY without**
> **causing harm to yourself or others.**

I was happy when I was with my wife because I enjoyed her company. I was happy when I was with my adult children because I enjoyed their company. I was happy at work because I enjoyed the intellectual stimulation and the thrill of discovering scientific breakthroughs. Experiencing a good family life and a good work life with accomplishments provided joy and a sense of fulfillment.

These are **<u>simple common-sense thoughts</u>** and it didn't take much time during the long flight to realize that this concept is valid.

I still had plenty of time on the flight and since I am a scientist, I had the urge to see if I could convert the qualitative concept of enjoying activities without causing harm into a quantitative parameter. After all, if we could measure happiness, we could then monitor changes in happiness and maybe come up with practical guidelines for how to **BE HAPPIER**.

That's how the rest of this book is structured:

1. Describe how to measure happiness.

2. Describe how to leverage your Happiness Score, and the related Opportunity Table, to make decisions to **BE HAPPIER**.

CHAPTER 5

How Can Happiness Be Measured? The Happiness Score

We established in the previous chapter that we want to maximize the time we engage in activities that we enjoy without causing harm. But, when you really think about it, the practical reality is that we can't experience joy and fulfillment 100% of the time.

For example, I don't enjoy washing dishes. I don't enjoy paying bills. I don't enjoy using the bathroom.

But we have no choice. We must pay bills or the electric company will shut off our electricity. We must use the bathroom because the law of conservation of matter dictates that if we do not eliminate solid and liquid waste from our bodies on a periodic basis, we will explode!

So, there must be at least two categories of what we do with our time. One category consists of time during which we are engaged in an activity that **we enjoy that does not cause harm**. A second category consists of time during which we are engaged in an activity that **we do NOT enjoy but would cause harm if we didn't do it**.

Those two categories still do not cover all the activities we do. What about sleep? What about if we are angry and yelling at a friend or family?

In the end, I divided time into **four** categories according to what we do with our time which in turn is the basis for characterizing and measuring happiness.

The four categories are defined as follows:

"INVEST time" is time during which we are engaged in activity that we enjoy that does not cause harm.

"SPEND time" is time during which we are engaged in activity that we do **NOT** enjoy, but would cause harm if we didn't do it.

"WASTE time" is time during which we are engaged in activity that causes harm, whether to ourselves or others.

"SLEEP" is sleep. You are either sleeping (or going to sleep) or not sleeping (or not going to sleep).

The words in these definitions have been chosen carefully.

In later chapters, each category will be discussed in detail. For now, let's introduce the "Happiness Score" metric and see how it is calculated.

Some of you do not like fractions or formulas. Don't let that get in the way. This equation is very simple. First, I'll explain the concept in words.

As you know, time marches on. It doesn't matter if you are enjoying yourself, not enjoying yourself or causing harm, the clock is still ticking!

The clock was ticking for millennia before you were born and the clock will keep on ticking for millennia after you're gone. Time is irreversible. You might not like this reality, but you might as well make the most of each second of your life from this very moment until the end of your days on earth because time is marching on, **with or without your happiness**!

> **It doesn't matter if you are enjoying yourself,**
> **not enjoying yourself or causing harm.**
> **The clock is still ticking!**

In order to understand the Happiness Score, you must first accept the fact that the clock is ticking all the time.

HAPPINESS SCORE POINTS

When you INVEST time, the clock is ticking and you **<u>get one point</u>** for every second that you are engaged in an activity that you enjoy without causing harm.

When you SPEND time, the clock is ticking and you **don't get any points** when you are engaged in an activity that you DON'T enjoy that would cause harm if you didn't do it.

When you WASTE time, the clock is ticking and you **lose one point** for every second during which you are engaged in an activity that causes harm to you or others.

The total amount of your waking hours (in seconds) is the total of the time you INVEST, SPEND and WASTE.

SLEEP is very important. However, we do not include SLEEP in the Happiness Score equation because you can't make choices or change behavior when you are asleep. As we will see later, the key to **BE HAPPIER** is to make choices and take actions that will directly affect your happiness. You can only make those decisions and take actions when you are conscious (awake).

The Happiness Score equation is shown in the diagram below.

For those of you who prefer to understand the calculation in words, here it is. To determine your Happiness Score, first deduct your WASTE time points from your INVEST time points to get your net positive points, which us arithmetic geeks call the "numerator" or top part of the fraction. Then divide that number by your total waking hour points (Invest + Spend + Waste; this is the denominator or the bottom part of the fraction). Then multiply by 100 to obtain your Happiness Score.

I know that some of you might not like fractions or equations, but I urge you to read the previous paragraph again until you understand it. It's actually very simple and the equation really only consists of one subtraction, one addition, one division and one multiplication. It's not that hard and the Happiness Score is the basis for this entire book and is the foundation for you to be able to make decisions and take action to **BE HAPPIER**.

HAPPINESS SCORE EQUATION

$$\frac{\text{Invest} - \text{Waste}}{\text{Invest} + \text{Spend} + \text{Waste}} \times 100$$

(waking hours measured in seconds)

Your Happiness Score goes UP when you INVEST time.

Your Happiness Score goes DOWN when you SPEND time.

Your Happiness Score goes DOWN A LOT MORE when you WASTE time.

Think about that for a moment. That's the way happiness should work in reality. You're happier when you are enjoying yourself without causing harm. You're not as happy when you're not enjoying yourself while having no choice. You should be less happy when you are harming yourself or others.

That is exactly what this equation does!

EXAMPLES

Let's illustrate with some examples. To simplify the arithmetic, we will refer to time in hours instead of seconds.

There are 168 hours in a week (7 days times 24 hours per day).

Let's say that you sleep about 48 hours per week (nearly 7 hours per night). That leaves you with 120 waking hours each week. The question is 'What do you do during those 120 hours per week?'

It's important to realize that the weekdays are different than the weekends since most people (not all) have more flexibility on the weekend to choose more enjoyable activities. That is why we will discuss time and activities in the following examples on a weekly basis and not a daily basis.

Example 1: Ideal Life

In an ideal life, which in reality is impossible, you would engage in only two types of activities: (1) activities you enjoy without causing harm and (2) sleep.

In this unrealistic ideal life, your Happiness Score would be a perfect 100 because every activity you do while not sleeping would be INVEST time.

Let's calculate. There are 168 hours in a week. If you sleep 48 hours during the entire week and you enjoy everything during the other 120 hours of the week, then your Happiness Score would be 100 as shown for the Ideal Life in the left column in the following table:

Happiness Scores for Three Hypothetical Scenarios

	Ideal Life ------------------ hours per week	Enjoy Home Life Don't Enjoy Work ------------------ hours per week	Don't Enjoy Home Life Don't Enjoy Work ------------------ hours per week
INVEST	120	70	20
SPEND	0	45	86
WASTE	0	5	20
SLEEP	48	48	42
Happiness Score	100	54	0

If you don't like fractions, skip this paragraph and the next table. For those of you who like to see calculations and fractions, the following table enables you to confirm your correct understanding of how the Happiness Score works.

	Ideal Life	Enjoy Home Life Don't Enjoy Work	Don't Enjoy Home Life Don't Enjoy Work
Fractions	$\dfrac{120 - 0}{120 + 0 + 0}$	$\dfrac{70 - 5}{70 + 45 + 5}$	$\dfrac{20 - 20}{20 + 86 + 20}$
Happiness Score	100	54	0

Remember that these are just three hypothetical scenarios. In reality, there are infinite combinations of time to INVEST, SPEND, WASTE and SLEEP. That means that your Happiness Score can be any number up to 100. In fact, your Happiness Score can even be negative, if you WASTE more time than INVEST time.

Is it possible to achieve a perfect score of 100? The practical answer is no, because even if you are super rich and you can pay people to do almost everything you don't enjoy (e.g., paying people or machines to wash dishes, or a bookkeeper to pay bills), there are still activities you must do yourself that you can't avoid, like certain personal hygiene activities.

So, even if you are a perfectionist with very high expectations and goals, don't be pressured to set your Happiness Score goal to be 100. It can't be done. That also means that if you are not a perfectionist, don't feel inadequate that your score is less than 100, because no one else has a perfect life (despite what they may post on social media).

Example 2: Enjoy Home Life, Don't Enjoy Work

A staggering number of adults do not enjoy their work.

While this will be discussed later in detail in Chapter 13, only a small minority of workers love their jobs. What about the rest of us? One of the major factors for job dissatisfaction is the worker's boss. Millions of bosses are often inadequately trained to manage. While some people enjoy their work, workplace, co-workers and bosses, many people don't.

Are you one of the many people who is not engaged in your work and/or would change bosses if given the opportunity?

> **If you don't enjoy your work life,**
> **you are SPENDING time at work!**

If you don't enjoy your work life, you are SPENDING time at work because if you didn't go to work you wouldn't have money to put food on the table, have a place to live or pay your phone bill. Remember that SPEND time means that you don't enjoy the activity but it would cause harm if you didn't do it. Not having enough money to cover your basic needs harms you.

Since most people work about 40 hours per week (1/3 of waking hours), people who SPEND their time at work can never achieve a Happiness Score of 67, even if they enjoy every other minute (i.e., all the rest is INVEST time and no WASTE time) and they have 120 waking hours per week.

If a person who enjoys their home life and doesn't enjoy work, commutes to work 30 minutes each way which they don't enjoy, 5 days each week, that's another 5 hours of SPEND time per week. The total SPEND time in this case is 45 hours per week (40 hours SPEND time at work + 5 hours SPEND time commuting).

When a person doesn't enjoy their job and the commute, they might be irritable when they get home which may cause friction with those at home (harm) which in turn could easily result in 5 hours per week of WASTE time.

Let's calculate. This person SPENDS 45 hours per week at work and the commute, WASTES 5 hours per week causing harm to others and enjoys every other minute of the week which equates to 70 hours of INVEST time. Then their Happiness Score is 54 (see the middle columns in the two tables above)

Is the Happiness Score of 54 just a number that we measure for curiosity? No. This relatively low Happiness Score of 54 should result in a self-call to action and you may choose to engage in some career planning as a major priority. We will dedicate an entire chapter later in this book (Chapter 13) to this specific topic of changes at work. In particular, we will provide guidelines and exercises to help you identify types of work you might enjoy.

Example 3: Don't Enjoy Home Life, Don't Enjoy Work

There is good news and bad news.

The good news is that the divorce rate in the US in recent years has decreased below the roughly 50% rate in the 1980s. The bad news is that it is still high. For first marriages, 42-45% will eventually terminate in divorce as the result. The recent divorce rates for second marriages and third marriages were 60% and 73%, respectively.[3]

Interestingly, the average age when couples commence the divorce process is 30 years old. This will have positive ramifications on making course corrections that will be discussed later in Chapter 12.

If a person does not enjoy their home life AND does not enjoy their work life, that doesn't mean that there aren't moments of enjoyment. There is always Sunday afternoon football or NASCAR or girls' night out. But overall, this is not a happy existence.

Let's calculate. This person might INVEST 20 hours per week enjoying selected activities, WASTE 20 hours per week in conflict with family members and might SPEND 86 hours per week of waking hours at work and during the commute and home. With all the unhappiness, this person is likely to be sleeping less, say 42 hours per week. According to the Happiness Score formula, this unhappy existence scores ZERO (see right column in the two tables above).

---

[3] https://canterburylawgroup.com/divorce-statistics-rates/

While this Happiness Score of zero is a major cause for concern and might even be depressing, the good news is that there is a lot of room for improvement. In fact, as changes are made by that person, progress can be monitored and celebrated at each milestone, say every 5 or 10 points.

You now realize that the Happiness Score and its continuous automatic measurement using the app "**Be Happier**," is a valuable tool (in some cases, a *crucial* tool) to help improve life. That is the whole point of this book, to **BE HAPPIER**!

How can we use the Happiness Score to **BE HAPPIER**?

We will point you in the right direction in the next chapter, "The Roadmap to Be Happier - Introduction" and we will show you how to identify specific opportunities to **BE HAPPIER** in Chapter 18, "How to Use the Opportunity Table to **BE HAPPIER**."

Following the introduction to the roadmap, we will invest chapters to describe in more detail the essence of each one of the categories of INVEST time, SPEND time, WASTE time and we will even clarify SLEEP.

Once armed with the full understanding of INVEST time, SPEND time and WASTE time, we will suggest for your consideration potential actions and concepts you can choose to implement for typical crucial strategic decisions that will enable you to **BE HAPPIER**, if you choose to improve your life.

Again, the choice to **BE HAPPIER** and improve your life is yours and **YOURS ONLY**. You must take responsibility for your happiness and that almost always requires making decisions and taking action.

Sometimes those decisions involve risk. That is why we very strongly recommend consulting with appropriate licensed professionals to assess and make recommendations for your specific individual situation before taking action. This is especially true **if the risk involves safety**, such as detaching from an abusive relationship. You should consult with appropriate licensed professionals to assess your specific situation and make recommendations about how to proceed **SAFELY**. You also need to ensure your safety during your process of seeking advice from licensed professionals.

Other risks include financial risk, such as when changing jobs or even when changing occupations, especially if you don't have a financial cushion to see you through to your desired transition. Again, you should consult with licensed professionals to assess your specific situation and make recommendations about how to proceed SAFELY.

In the next chapters, we will embark on the journey to **BE HAPPIER**.

Summary – The Happiness Score

- **"INVEST** time" is time during which you are engaged in activity that you enjoy that does not cause harm to you and/or others.

- **"SPEND** time" is time during which you are engaged in activity that you do **NOT** enjoy but would cause harm if you didn't do it.

- **"WASTE** time" is time during which you are engaged in activity that causes harm, fear or pain to you and/or others.

- **"SLEEP"** is sleep. You are either sleeping (or going to sleep) or not sleeping (or not going to sleep).

- The clock is ticking whether you are enjoying, not enjoying or causing harm.

- Your Happiness Score increases every second you INVEST, decreases every second you SPEND and decreases a lot every second you WASTE.

- You have probably figured out already by yourself that in order to **BE HAPPIER**, you need to maximize INVEST time and minimize both SPEND time and WASTE time.

- The free app "**Be Happier**" will track your Happiness Score automatically with only 2-8 taps per day when you transition from enjoying what you're doing to not enjoying or causing harm.

- If you need to make changes in your life to **BE HAPPIER** that involve risk, especially safety-related risks, you must ensure your safety first, even when seeking the help of appropriate licensed professionals such as psychologists, social workers, financial advisors and others. If you or someone you know is struggling or in crisis, help is available. In the United States, call or text 988 or chat 988lifeline.org (988 Suicide & Crisis Lifeline).

CHAPTER 6

The Roadmap to Be Happier

You might have already figured out that in order to **BE HAPPIER**, you need to convert SPEND time and WASTE time into INVEST time as much as possible.

In other words, you need to first identify the activities that you do not enjoy or are causing harm that are right now a part of your daily life and then make changes so that you will enjoy that time without causing harm.

Let's illustrate with an example.

Let's say that you drive 30 minutes to your current workplace every day. Traffic is heavy and you don't enjoy the drive. If indeed you must drive to work in order to do your job (regardless of whether you enjoy your work or not), you are currently SPENDING time during the drive to work.

One crucial concept in this book and the roadmap to **BE HAPPIER** is that when you catch yourself SPENDING time (or when the app "**Be Happier**" shows you that you are SPENDING time), you should ask yourself the question 'What can I do right now, or in the future, to convert this activity from **not enjoying it to enjoying it without causing harm?**' We call this the "**SPEND-to-INVEST Question.**"

The roadmap to **BE HAPPIER** requires that you ask yourself the SPEND-to-INVEST question at the beginning of every activity for which you SPEND time.

> **When you SPEND time, ask yourself the question**
> **'What can I do right now, or in the future, to**
> **convert this activity from *not enjoying it to***
> ***enjoying it without causing harm?*'**

In theory, you should also ask this question when you WASTE time, but your reality when you are causing harm (yelling or violence, for example) is such that your thoughts are likely too preoccupied with emotion or safety concerns to be able to focus on asking and resolving questions that require critical thinking in parallel. In those cases, you can analyze your conversion of WASTE time to less harmful activities after the situation calms down.

Let's make a list of some potential answers to the SPEND-to-INVEST Question for SPENDING time for the activity of driving to work. As you review this list, you will recognize that some of the potential answers are easy and practical to implement. In contrast, some answers will require a major life change that takes too much time, discomfort, upheaval and/or resources to be practical unless you are very committed to resolving the problem. **YOU** get to choose how much effort you want to invest to resolve a given SPEND time challenge.

Following are some potential answers and modifications to convert SPEND time driving to work into INVEST time driving to work:

- Listen to non-distracting enjoyable music during the drive (as long as it is safe).

- Listen to non-distracting comedy during the drive (as long as it is safe).

- Listen to non-distracting podcasts during the drive (as long as it is safe).

- Listen to non-distracting audiobooks during the drive (as long as it is safe).

- Convince your boss to allow you to work from home 1-5 days/week.

- Change your work schedule to avoid rush hour (7a-3p versus 9a-5p).

- Buy or rent an alternative residence so you can move closer to your workplace that will reduce your commute time.

- Change your employer to one with a workplace closer to your current home or with a route to work that does not involve undesirable traffic (I once changed my employer located in urban Philadelphia to another employer located in semi-rural mid-Michigan).

- Change your primary occupation so you can work wherever you want, including from home (I did exactly that in 1995).

- Add your own practical or impractical ideas…

Clearly, some of these ideas near the top of the list require very minor modifications and zero resources while other ideas toward the bottom of the list might require such an upheaval of your current life, that they may be impractical. Do you really want to retrain for a completely different job or occupation? Do you really want to take any necessary risks? Would you want to move clear across the country? The beauty of asking the SPEND-to-INVEST Question and writing down hypothetical answers is that you get to choose which modification(s) suit you and your situation the best!

It's YOUR life. You get to choose. Do you want to **BE HAPPIER**?

How many minutes do you think it would take to make a list of hypothetical answers to a SPEND-to-INVEST Question? Usually, not many.

If you invest 10 minutes to write down 5-10 hypothetical answers to a SPEND-to-INVEST Question like the one above for driving to work, and you wind up not changing anything in your life, were those 10 minutes a waste of time? Probably not.

On the other hand, let's calculate the return on your investment of 10 minutes to write down 5-10 hypothetical answers to a SPEND-to-INVEST Question if you DO make a change. If the change enables you to convert 5 hours per week of driving from SPEND time to INVEST time for just the next 10 years, you would convert 2,500 SPEND hours of your life into INVEST hours!

Wow! That demonstrates the power of investing 10 minutes to analyze just one SPEND time activity to convert 2,500 hours (150,000 minutes) of your future irreversible life to **BE HAPPIER**!

Now imagine how many more thousands or tens of thousands of hours, **of your future irreversible life** you could convert from SPEND time to enjoyable INVEST time, if only you would sit down with yourself and analyze the numerous life activities you currently perform that you don't enjoy!

Are you now curious or even motivated to identify activities in your CURRENT daily life that you could change from SPEND to INVEST?! If so, then the exercise in Chapter 8 of this book that focuses on SPEND time may outstandingly justify the time you INVEST reading this book and/or downloading the free app "**Be Happier**."

If you are very committed to identifying activities in your CURRENT daily life that you could change from SPEND to INVEST, you will greatly appreciate the extremely practical tool called the "Opportunity Table" that we will describe in Chapter 18!

If you think this analysis is hypothetical or silly, consider the following real situation that has so far affected 700 hours of my happiness. I live in New Jersey. My 93-year-old mother lives in a senior living facility in Kentucky near my brother. The 708-mile drive from my house to Kentucky is long and laborious.

When I'm in a hurry, I fly from Philadelphia to Louisville and rent a car for the few days of my visit. However, I usually drive. One day several years ago, the GPS app recommended that I drive through the beautiful country scenery of western Maryland and West Virginia instead of on the mostly monotonous Pennsylvania Turnpike and the long relatively flat sections of highway in southern Ohio. What a beautiful trip! I discovered that I love the road hours in West Virginia, especially the gorgeous winding drive on I-79 between Morgantown, WV and Charleston, WV.

I decided to convert my 708-mile drive from SPEND time drudgery to INVEST time enjoyment. I now look forward to the 10.5 road hours when I drive to see my mother every 2-3 months. I listen to comedy, music, podcasts and I schedule calls with my customers and colleagues who I enjoy the most! I proactively made this choice and I am so much happier now.

In addition, if something stressful happens before my drive, I use the 10.5 road hours, much of which is driving through the scenic mountains, to relieve that stress. If something stressful happens when I'm in Kentucky (like when my father was in hospice and passed away in Louisville in 2018), I use the drive time to reflect and recover before reentering reality at home in New Jersey. The scenic mountain drive is much more therapeutic than my ability to cope and readjust during a short 2-hour flight from Louisville to Philadelphia.

I am not saying that every single event of SPEND time can be converted into INVEST time. What I am saying is that if we can convert even half of our SPEND time into INVEST time, our Happiness Score will increase because that is the way the remarkably simple Happiness Score equation is designed. Imagine the positive impact on your happiness for the rest of your life!

Is it worth a few minutes of analysis to ask and answer in writing the SPEND-to-INVEST Question for the 5-10 activities in your daily life for which you SPEND time? Absolutely!

I cannot emphasize enough the importance of this question of converting SPEND time into INVEST time! If you really want to improve your life and **BE HAPPIER**, especially if you are SPENDING (not enjoying) any given activity more than 10 hours per week, you will likely be asking yourself this SPEND-to-INVEST Question often when you first start taking this concept seriously.

In fact, if you find yourself asking the SPEND-to-INVEST Question daily or multiple times per day in the next few weeks, that will **trigger you to realize that you that you are on your way to improving your life!** Moreover, if you answer the SPEND-to-INVEST Question with a solution from time to time and you are using the app "**Be Happier**," you will **actually see your progress in your Happiness Score every time you check the app!** Why? Because when you convert SPEND time into INVEST time, the equation for the Happiness Score firmly dictates that your Happiness Score *MUST* increase. It is purposely designed that way.

The feedback of watching your Happiness Score increase is an incredibly highly motivating factor and you will want to increase your Happiness Score even more! Monitoring your Happiness Score will motivate you to modify your behavior!

> **Monitoring your Happiness Score will motivate you to modify your behavior and BE HAPPIER!**

Remember, increasing your happiness is not a competitive sport. Increasing your Happiness Score is very personal to you because it has a direct impact on how happy you really are! The app "**Be Happier**" can really affect the rest of your life and it's free. Remember that the app does not collect any of your personal information. Your happiness is between you and yourself. No one will know except you (unless you decide to share your progress with an accountability partner who has no relationship with us).

The question that remains is "Are you willing to now take control of your happiness and convert SPEND time into INVEST time as the clock keeps ticking towards the end of your life?"

I would like to add a general comment here. Since you are reading this self-help book, you are most likely seeking to improve your life and you are open-minded to concepts and methods that will help. If so, then chances are that your desired improvements from self-help are heavily weighted toward **converting SPEND time into INVEST time** and LESS toward **converting WASTE time into INVEST time**. Why? Because good people in search of self-improvement (like you?) are less likely to be causing massive amounts of harm. That may not always be true, but it usually is.

Of course, you definitely want to minimize WASTE time. But most people who are sincere about self-help are not causing harm during the majority of their time. While some people are causing harm almost all the time, those few people are usually not reading self-help books to bring joy to themselves and to the rest of the world.

So, the good news is that you are likely poised for success even if your Happiness Score is lower than it can be because it's usually easier to "fix" SPEND time than WASTE time, if you are a person who doesn't cause much harm to others.

Now that we have covered the basics of the Happiness Score and introduced you to the SPEND-to-INVEST Question, let's take a deeper dive in the next chapters into each of the four categories of INVEST, SPEND, WASTE and SLEEP.

SUMMARY - The roadmap to **BE HAPPIER** requires that you:

1. Become aware of each of the **specific activities** in which you SPEND time and WASTE time. The app "**Be Happier**" is a free tool to make this easy!

2. Become aware of the **number of hours** you SPEND time and WASTE time for each specific activity in Item 1 above. The app "**Be Happier**" is a free tool to make this easy!

3. Identify and prioritize potential solutions to convert SPEND time and WASTE time to INVEST time.

4. Implement practical solutions from Item 3 above (if safe).

5. Monitor the increase in your Happiness Score.

6. Celebrate minor improvements and major victory milestones as your Happiness Score increases.

7. Recognize and enjoy your increased happiness!

CHAPTER 7

INVEST Time

We defined INVEST time as "time during which we are engaged in an activity that we **enjoy and does not cause harm**." In this chapter, we will explore in more detail what INVEST time is like in real life. We will also address situations that might look like INVEST but are really WASTE.

First, we should recognize that different people enjoy different things. That's totally OK and perfectly natural. For example, I am a chemist and I love talking about organic chemistry while most people hate organic chemistry! I don't eat fruit, although many people consider it a real treat. We all enjoy different activities.

That means that there is no universal list of activities for all of us that must fall into the INVEST time category. In fact, one of the major advantages of the extremely simple Happiness Score equation and the very nature of the definition of INVEST time, is that it is **totally customizable for every person on the planet**.

Even though different people enjoy different activities, the next page shows a list of suggested activities from which you can choose to create your own customizable list for INVEST time. I strongly encourage you to put in writing a list of YOUR enjoyable activities to remind you how to enjoy your life more. Add your own enjoyable activities to this list. Write in the margins of this book if you must.

I once took a course for aspiring entrepreneurs at Wharton Business School (10 hours for only $50 in 1992!) and the instructor, who was wearing a suit and tie, tried to convince us to write a formal business plan by saying **"IF IT AIN'T WRIT, IT AIN'T THUNK!"** I agree wholeheartedly with this statement and I strongly urge you to INVEST a few minutes in writing YOUR personal customized list of activities that you enjoy that do not cause harm.

Do it NOW! I'll wait.

I speculate that you just kept on reading and didn't make the list. I'm serious. Please make the list and put it IN WRITING! As always, ensure your safety if the discovery of this list by others could pose a safety risk.

In order to encourage you to get started, turn one page ahead and you will find a space to create your own personal list of activities you enjoy that do not cause harm. Write down FIVE (at least!) and WRITE THEM **NOW**!!!

INVEST TIME ACTIVITIES LIST

(Examples of activities that you might enjoy that do not cause harm)

Add and delete activities on this list to create YOUR OWN INVEST TIME LIST.

- Engaging in quality time with family
- Engaging in quality time with friends
- Eating a good healthy meal
- Cooking
- Listening to music
- Playing a musical instrument
- Singing
- Dancing
- Learning
- Exercising and playing sports
- Meditating or praying

- Participating in clubs (e.g., book club) or special interest groups
- Volunteering
- Mentoring or teaching
- Reading
- Reading to children
- Fishing
- Hiking
- Camping
- Being a leader in Boy Scouts/Girl Scouts
- Traveling
- Creating art
- Studying art
- Gardening
- Engaging in a craft (e.g., quilting, building furniture, etc.)
- Engaging in meaningful intimate relations (safely)
- Work (only if you enjoy your occupation)
- Add your own: _____
- Add your own: _____
- Add your own: _____
- Add your own: _____
- Add your own: _____

OPPORTUNITY LIST TO INVEST TIME

_____

(Fill in your name)

Following are activities that **I** enjoy that do not cause harm

_____

_____

_____

_____

_____

_____

_____

_____

_____

_____

_____

_____

RE-PROGRAMMING YOUR BRAIN: INVEST VS SPEND

When you first read the definitions of INVEST time and SPEND time in Chapter 5, you were probably resistant to the use of these words. Why? Because my definitions are not what you were taught over the years.

Let's face it, EVERYONE says "spend time."

I hate the word "spend!"

After you hear the explanation, I'm hoping that you will eliminate the word "spend" from your vocabulary about 95% of the time, like I have done since 2007 when I invented this formula as the model for the Happiness Score.

Let's consider two common usages of the word "spend." Notice that I stopped capitalizing the words "spend" in the last few sentences…this was done intentionally.

Common Question #1: How much time did you spend on the beach when you went on vacation?

Common Question #2: How much was US government spending in 2021?

I will address Common Question #2 first. Please know that I am experiencing a gut-knotting physical reaction as I am writing these sentences using the disgusting word "spend!"

A moment ago, I typed in the search box of a common search engine "US government spending 2021." I quickly learned that the number was $10.04 trillion. Why am I telling you this? Because the search engine clearly recognized the term "government spending" and the URLs (see screenshot below) of the first two hits at the top of the pages were:

- https://www.usaspending.gov/
- https://usgovernmentspending.com/

Now I will type in the search line "US government **investing** 2021." The disturbing results are shown in the screenshot below. It's worse than I expected!

Let's compare. When I typed the search term "US government **spending** 2021" in the first search, I got a variety of reasonable options for government spending. They included plain government spending, a pie chart of government spending, US spending or federal spending. The search engine had no problem at all understanding the term "government spending" and spitting out thousands of relevant hits in a microsecond!

In contrast, when I typed the search term "US government **investing** 2021" in the second search, **the search engine thought I was nuts** (!) because the combination of the words "government" and "investing" is a sequence that NEVER happens. You're thinking the same thing too since you have never heard the word combination **government investing**. It's ALWAYS **government spending**!

You see, when our elected officials get our tax money, they **SPEND IT!** They DON'T INVEST IT!!!!!

The money is theirs to SPEND. They throw a few billion here and they throw a few billion there. They SPEND our tax money. They DON'T INVEST our tax money.

The vocabulary we use in our minds determines how we behave!!!!

If we renamed "government **spending**" to "government **investing**," maybe we could hold our elected officials more accountable, because the word **INVEST** implies a **RETURN ON INVESTMENT!**

When you INVEST money, you expect something in return. When you SPEND money, it's gone and who cares?

I think that we should chastise politicians every time they utter the words "government spending" and we should somehow inject them with feel-good endorphins every time they utter the words "government investing."

Do you think I'm kidding? I'm not.

The vocabulary we use in our minds determines our behavior.

Before returning to happiness, I would like to share another use of the word INVEST versus SPEND to drive this crucial point deep into your mind.

I am a national speaker who presents a lot of lectures on the topic of part-time real estate investing (www.PartTimeInvestors.com) and I am an international speaker who presents a lot of lectures on the topic of phase-transfer catalysis (www.PhaseTransferCatalysis.com), in more than 300 cities in 39 countries so far.

After I came up with the Happiness Score and the definitions of INVEST, SPEND and WASTE in 2007, I started asking my real estate investor audiences 'By a show of hands, how many **real estate spenders** do we have in the audience?' The response is usually total silence with people starting to look at each other with puzzled looks on their faces. So, I repeat the question a second time 'How many **real estate spenders** do we have in the audience?'. Eventually, someone blurts out 'What do you mean?!'

I then say, 'I'm sorry, let me correct myself. By a show of hands, how many **real estate investors** are in the room?' Everyone raises their hand. I then explain that we INVEST money in real estate because we expect a return on our investment. We don't SPEND money when we buy, fix and sell or rent real estate. We INVEST money. I add that SPENDING money in real estate sounds pretty stupid and that is why they had puzzled looks on their faces when I asked **real estate spenders** to raise their hands.

The word combination "real estate spender" sounds as ridiculous as the word combination "fall up." Right?

I then ask the audience, "How much do you typically spend on replacing a water heater in a rental unit." Within one second, I usually hear 3-10 people shout out $1,000 or another similar amount. At the same time, I scan the audience and I always find one intelligent person smiling. I call on that quick learner and I then ask, "Why are you smiling?" and that person always responds with the same exact words, even in different audiences "We don't **SPEND** money on a water heater, we **INVEST** money in a water heater."

I then quickly ask the audience in as nonchalant a voice as possible "By the way, how much do you typically spend on a granite countertop?" There is always one person who throws out a number and five people yell out "Don't you get it? You **INVEST** in a countertop, you don't **SPEND** money on a countertop!"

I have been training people for a decade and a half, one audience at a time, to stop using the highly inappropriate word "spend" and substitute it with the word INVEST. It's important to say what we mean because the words we use govern our behavior. Politicians say that they "spend" money but they are really WASTING billions of dollars of real money. Real estate investors INVEST money, especially mom-and-pop investors (like me) because we cannot afford to waste any money at all.

Now, let's get back to happiness.

Children learn language because their parents talk to them from the moment they are born. As parents, we do this instinctively even though we know that a newborn doesn't understand language and can't talk at birth.

From the moment each of my grandchildren was born, I started asking them if they would like to **<u>INVEST</u>** time with me!

I programmed my grandchildren that the word combinations "INVEST time with me" or "INVEST quality time with me," are normal, naturally flowing word combinations.

My grandchildren would look at me with a puzzled face if I asked them if they want to "**spend** time with me." Since my grandkids could talk, the word combination "**spend** time with their grandfather" sounded as stupid to them as the word combination "**fall up**."

As they have been growing up, they have known for absolute sure that they INVEST quality time with their grandparents. They sleep over at our house almost every weekend with what they termed "no mommy-daddy nights" since they were about 2 years old, which is about the same time that the internal language in their minds already understood that they INVEST quality time with us. "**Spend** quality time" is a phrase that makes no sense.

Yes, we see our grandchildren almost every weekend for a sleepover (the oldest is now 11 years old) and I can honestly say that **I <u>never</u> SPEND any quality time with my grandchildren!** I always INVEST time with my grandchildren!

In fact, my grandchildren are now so deeply programmed that they correct their friends when their friends use the word "spend" to describe time they enjoy or money they INVEST on items they enjoy.

If you agree with this thought process here are a few phrases that should be **cringeworthy** to you from this moment forward for the rest of your life:

- **spend** quality time with family
- government **spending**
- real estate **spenders**
- fall **up** (already cringeworthy)

It is very embarrassing to say this, but I let an inappropriate four-letter word slip out of my mouth occasionally more than the word SPEND. I don't curse often because it is uncomfortable using bad words. But using one of George Carlin's "7-words-you-can't-say-on-TV" is not as uncomfortable to me as the knot in my stomach if I actually slip up and say the word SPEND while referring to either money or time. The exception is for situations in which I MUST engage in an activity that I do not enjoy but would cause harm if I didn't do it (SPEND), such as paying bills, washing dishes or using the bathroom.

By the way, how much money did you spend on your last vacation?

Hopefully, you smiled to yourself and said, "Not one penny." If so, you have now been reprogrammed to enjoy your life more and **BE HAPPIER!**

This is proof that you can change your outlook and subsequently change your performance, by accepting the definition of INVEST time and INVEST money while rejecting the internal language that causes people to **spend** time (ugh!) and **spend** money (ugh!) unless there is absolutely no other choice.

In contrast, my search for the term "government investing" baffled the search engine, forcing it to attempt to figure out what I REALLY meant. Although it found millions of results for "government spending," it could not find one instance of "government investing." After frantically guessing "government bonds," it then decided that I must have been so absurdly mistaken when I used the word "government" with "investing" that it returned "How America invests 2021," completely omitting government from the entire conversation!

It is sad how the inappropriate use of the word SPEND in society causes WASTE instead of INVEST!

You have progressed a lot in the last few minutes of reading! Congratulations!

> **Every time you are about to slip up and utter the word "spend" when referring to time or money, take a 1-second pause from your audible talking and ask yourself the question "do I mean INVEST or WASTE?" Then continue your sentence out loud.**

By the way, ChatGPT is an AI platform that started in December 2022. In February 2023, I asked ChatGPT "How much was US government investing in 2021?" and it responded "It's difficult to provide a specific figure for total government investment in 2021, as investment can take many forms, including grants, loans, tax incentives, and contracts. However, in recent years, federal investment in research and development has averaged about $150 billion per year." When I asked ChatGPT the same exact question with one word changed "how much was US government spending in 2021?" it responded with the numbers of trillions of dollars from the Congressional Budget Office (CBO). Yes, in February 2023, ChatGPT knew that humans mean one thing when they ask for **government spending** and something completely different when they ask for **government investing**!

Let's take it a step further and have you make numerous value judgements every single day that will cause you to **BE HAPPIER**. I submit the following recommendation for your strong consideration.

For example, let's say your partner asks you "Where are you going, honey?" and you're about to say "I'm going out to spend time with my friends at the bar." Before you utter the word "spend" ask yourself if you intend to INVEST time and enjoy time with your friends having a beer and not causing harm, or do you intend to WASTE time and get plastered with 5 beers followed by 3 shots of whiskey at the bar, then maybe drive home drunk and kill yourself or others unintentionally?

It's now been more than 15 years since I have been audibly pausing when I'm about to use the word SPEND and make a quick judgment call if I really intend to INVEST time (or money) or WASTE time (or money). I practice what I preach. I strongly encourage you to do the same. After a few weeks, you'll get used to the realization that SPEND is the new S-word. You'll see!

WHAT ABOUT INVEST VERSUS WASTE?

The reality is that when you're enjoying yourself, quite a few situations could go either way, INVEST or WASTE. <u>The difference is a decision that could potentially result in harm</u>. I urge you to read that last sentence again.

Following are some examples that could be INVEST or WASTE depending on your decisions. Remember that in order to **BE HAPPIER**, reflected in a higher Happiness Score, we must increase INVEST time, which means we increase the number of seconds we enjoy **<u>WITHOUT CAUSING HARM</u>**!

- Eating a good meal
  - o INVEST = eating healthy food
  - o WASTE = eating unhealthy food consistently or excessively

- Drinking alcohol with friends
  - o INVEST = 1-2 beers before karaoke
  - o WASTE = getting drunk then driving

- Watching TV
  - INVEST = winding down after an intense day or week at work
  - WASTE = watching TV instead of eating dinner with your family or reading a book to your kids at bedtime

- Posting or reading social media
  - INVEST = winding down after an intense day at work, promoting your business or community service events
  - WASTE = cyberbullying, posting disinformation, maliciously attacking people's political or religious views

- Playing video games
  - INVEST = winding down after an intense day at work or study
  - WASTE = playing instead of doing homework or feeding a gaming addiction to the exclusion of family, work or sleep

I happen to watch a lot of television. In fact, I have seen every episode of Andy Griffith at least 7 times. Really. To me, the lighthearted plots, almost devoid of serious problems, are like listening to serene classical music. However, I am usually working while I watch Andy Griffith. Whether I am watching Andy Griffith, NASCAR, sitcoms or Sunday afternoon football, TV does not interfere with my productivity. When the grandchildren stay with us, I never isolate myself in front of the television. In other words, watching TV or video gaming can be INVEST time or WASTE time, depending on whether or not you are causing harm to yourself or others.

WHAT ABOUT DIFFERENT LEVELS OF JOY AND FULFILLMENT FOR DIFFERENT ACTIVITIES?

Before moving on to Chapter 8 about SPEND time (where the most opportunity exists for increasing your Happiness Score), we need to ask the question about how to address different levels of enjoyment for different activities.

When we first started developing the app "**Be Happier**," we actually had three buttons for INVEST to reflect three levels of enjoyment which were "enjoy some," "enjoy" and "enjoy a lot." When we had three levels of enjoy, the Happiness Score equation gave half a point for each second that we "enjoy some," one point for each second that we "enjoy" (as we have in the current simple equation) and two points for each second that "we enjoy a lot."

Interestingly, when I presented the Happiness Score model to my 8-year-old grandson one week before starting to write this book, he actually perceptively suggested creating a scale for different levels of enjoyment since he said that he enjoys scoring a goal when playing soccer more than collecting Pokémon cards. I was amazed at how much an 8-year-old innately understood the quantitative aspects of happiness. I also am proud of his parents instilling in him and his 10-year-old sister at that time, the confidence to be able to challenge concepts presented by adults by applying critical thinking and logic to thought processes that may benefit from further optimization.

In the end, several reasons led to the tough decision to keep the definition of INVEST in its simplest form as "enjoy without causing harm" without allowing for varying levels of enjoyment.

The first reason resulted from thinking about the activities that we enjoy the most. These are activities during which the feel-good endorphins are flowing at their highest rate. Examples may include scoring a goal when playing a 90-minute soccer match, or the average amount of time during a 168-hour week that we safely engage in consensual intimate relations with our partner. Most of the activities that we rate at the highest level of enjoyment have relatively shorter durations than activities that we enjoy on a sustained basis.

If a person enjoys the essence of their work (like I do), then these 40 hours per week of joy and fulfillment out of 120 waking hours per week account for about 33 points. If we were to start ranking different activities at different levels of enjoyment, then an extra hour per week of an unusually high enjoyment activity, would add an extra one point to the Happiness Score.

It is important to understand that the Happiness Score is a useful empirical tool that can be leveraged to make decisions, but the Happiness Score is not intended to provide quantitative resolution with three significant digits of accuracy.

In addition and more importantly, if we were to introduce a ranking system for each level of joy and harm, there would be two extremely important negative ramifications which are **complexity** and **subjectivity**. I decided it was very important, in particular, to avoid subjectivity in order to avoid people lying to themselves and fudging their numbers. The Happiness Score model MUST be objectively valid in order for it to be useful. Objectivity is MUCH more important than three digits of accuracy versus two digits of accuracy.

The app "**Be Happier**" is designed to be used on the fly in your real-world life and any introduction of complexity would GREATLY reduce its user-friendliness. For example, let's say that you are at work and you enjoy the essence of the work and then you are called into a meeting with human resources to discuss changes to the company's healthcare plan. In the current version of the app, your clock is ticking in the INVEST category (green color screen) when you are enjoying your work, but when you enter the human resources meeting that you don't enjoy, you quickly take out your phone and click on the yellow SPEND button, slide your phone back into your pocket and continue your meeting. This minimizes disruption in your workflow.

In contrast, having to make a judgement call to rank every change of activity on a scale of 1 to 3, 1 to 5 or 1 to 10, for how much or how little you enjoy or don't enjoy every activity, would greatly interfere with the flow of your daily life. The subjectivity of your mood or judgment at that moment may even render the rating completely inaccurate.

One of the issues with the alternative methods for measuring happiness is that most of them require answering lengthy cumbersome questionnaires and self-reporting answers with ranking levels of happiness for each question. This may be practical to assess large populations to determine the Happiness Score of the population of entire countries once per year, but it is not practical for an individual to gage their own Happiness Score by themselves daily, continuously monitor their score and be able to see progress when they make changes in their personal lives.

The simplicity of our Happiness Score equation is a MAJOR benefit that makes it very practical for individual use, especially on a smartphone that is within reach of almost everyone 24/7. You only have to make ONE JUDGMENT at a time, which you do 2-8 times per day. That's it!

The judgment is:

1   Are you STARTING an activity that you enjoy without causing harm? ➜ Tap the green INVEST button.

2. Are you STARTING an activity that you do NOT enjoy but it would cause harm if you didn't do it? ➜ Tap the yellow SPEND button.

3. Are you STARTING to experience or cause harm? ➜ Tap the red WASTE button. Sometimes, you'll want to go back and add or edit this activity after the fact when it is safe or after you calm down.

4. Are you going to sleep? ➜ Tap the blue SLEEP button.

Prior to writing this book, I have been testing the app "**Be Happier**" for two years and it does not interfere with my daily flow of activities, but it DOES help me understand my baseline, what happens if I have a bad week or bad month and it alerts to me to changes I need to make to get back on track.

When we had six buttons in the app (3.5 years ago), which included an extra button for "enjoy some" and an extra button for "enjoy a lot," I was constantly having to interrupt the flow of my daily activities to make judgments about how much am I enjoying a certain activity and I found that it was disruptive and I was not making consistent judgement calls.

If I had to further rank the enjoyment of each activity on a scale of 1-5, it would have interrupted my daily activity flow too much and I would have been a slave to worrying about the app too much.

The conclusion was that in order for the Happiness Score to be practical and useful, the following criteria had to be met:

- The definitions of INVEST, SPEND, WASTE and SLEEP had to be simple, definitive and mutually exclusive so that instantaneous categorization can be made with little thought or interruption to daily activities.

- The resolution of the Happiness Score should have two significant digits so that it would be useful to monitor progress but three significant digits or more would require much more complexity and not add much incremental value for making better decisions.

To further justify simplicity over attempted accuracy (using two significant digits instead of three), it's useful to consider how we use the Happiness Score in our daily, weekly and monthly lives.

As will be explained in later chapters, the biggest impacts on Happiness Score for most people are:

- Choosing relationships (life partner and friends), which may account for as much as 40-50 points out of 100 and

- Choosing one's occupation (including place of employment or entrepreneurship), which may account for about 25-35 points out of 100, depending on one's individual situation.

The magnitudes of each of our life's various activities are such that quantifying the Happiness Score to two significant digits, strikes a good balance that is practical yet useful.

INVEST - Summary of key points

- INVEST time requires both enjoyment and causing no harm.

- Maximize INVEST time to **BE HAPPIER.**

- The Happiness Score is designed to increase as you increase your INVEST time.

- Time and life are irreversible, therefore consciously INVEST as much time as possible, remembering not to cause harm.

- Make a **written** list of INVEST time activities (if safe).

- Give names to each of your INVEST time activities, SPEND time activities and WASTE time activities in the app "**Be Happier.**"

- Ask yourself the SPEND-to-INVEST Question often.

- Never utter the word SPEND out loud (or even think that word in your mind) unless you are forced to do something you don't enjoy.

- Whenever you are about to slip up and say the word SPEND out loud, pause and ask yourself, do I mean INVEST or do I mean WASTE?

- WASTE time might be disguised as enjoyable INVEST time when it is really WASTE time because of harm being caused to you or others.

CHAPTER 8

SPEND Time

We defined SPEND time as "time during which we are engaged in an activity that we **do NOT enjoy, but would cause harm if we didn't do it**."

For most of you, the <u>biggest opportunity for you to increase your Happiness Score</u> and **BE HAPPIER** is "hidden" <u>right under your nose in the SPEND time category!</u>

If you want to **BE HAPPIER**, you should:

1. Identify activities on which you are SPENDING time.

2. Face your reality head-on and figure out potential solutions to convert SPEND time into INVEST time. Ask the SPEND-to-INVEST Question.

3. Make adjustments and **BE HAPPIER** for the rest of your life!

For roughly half of the population, the biggest potential to **BE HAPPIER** is related to their work. Those people are the ones who do NOT enjoy their workplace or occupation but need to go to work to make money to pay for basic needs such as food, shelter, clothing, utilities and other essentials. We will devote an entire chapter to this highly important topic of being happier at work (Chapter 13).

As we noted in Chapter 7 on INVEST time, everyone is different and everyone enjoys different activities. That applies to SPEND time as well. We cannot create a universal list of activities that accurately characterizes SPEND time for every person.

Even though different people have different sets of SPEND time activities, on the next pages we are providing a list of suggested activities from which you can choose to create your own customizable list for SPEND time activities. Remember that your customized SPEND time activity list is likely where your biggest opportunities exist to improve your life and increase your Happiness Score!

I strongly urge you to INVEST a few minutes (or SPEND them if you don't enjoy it!) to create in writing YOUR personal customized OPPORTUNITY LIST of activities that you do NOT enjoy that cause harm if you don't do them. As always, ensure your safety in case your written list is discovered.

Go to the next page and you will find a space to create your own personal OPPORTUNITY list of SPEND activities. Write down at least three and WRITE THEM **NOW**!!!

SPEND TIME ACTIVITIES LIST

(Examples of activities that you do not enjoy but would cause harm if you didn't do them)

Add and delete activities on this list to create YOUR OWN SPEND TIME LIST

- Paying bills
- Tax form preparation
- Driving to work
- Using the bathroom
- Changing diapers
- Preparing meals (when you don't enjoy cooking)
- Care giving
- Washing dishes, doing the laundry, cleaning house

- Fixing broken things around the house (when you don't enjoy this activity)

- Taking out the trash

- Mowing the lawn

- Shopping for food, fuel

- Interacting with immediate family members whose company you don't enjoy

- Work (if you DON'T enjoy your occupation or workplace)

- Taking required courses outside of your major in college or work-related continuing education

- Recovering from illness (unless creating value = INVEST time)

- Add your own: _____

- Add your own: _____

- Add your own: _____

- Add your own: _____

- Add your own: _____

> **The "lowest hanging fruit" opportunities**
> **to increase your Happiness Score and**
> **BE HAPPIER are often "hidden" right under**
> **your nose in the SPEND time category!**

OPPORTUNITY LIST TO REDUCE SPEND TIME

_____

(Fill in your name)

Following are activities that I **<u>CURRENTLY</u>** do **<u>NOT</u>** enjoy but would cause harm if I didn't do them

As will be seen in Chapter 13, the biggest, or second biggest, impact on the Happiness Score for people who do not enjoy their **WORK**, is to design and execute a practical path to change jobs and/or change occupations. If that is your situation, you will definitely want to read and actually study Chapter 13.

Another very important category for converting SPEND time into INVEST time is to analyze whether certain **RELATIONSHIPS** in your life fall into the category that you feel might be "I do not enjoy it but would cause harm if I wasn't in the relationship." Some relationships that you don't enjoy might seem to be necessary, but are they really? In two extreme cases, I detached contact with two toxic family members. It is not suggested here to disown family members whenever you face conflict. What is suggested is to analyze extremely toxic relationships (WASTE time) with selected family and friends and very carefully consider whether the relationship is actually harmful, not just "not enjoyable." Happiness in relationships will be addressed in Chapter 12.

While relationships and work dominate people's Happiness Score, make no mistake, you can improve your life and increase your Happiness Score by making many small decisions in the routines of your life.

Driving was covered in Chapter 6 as an example of how to convert SPEND time into INVEST time.

Sometimes money may be needed to convert SPEND time into INVEST time. For example, you can outsource mowing the lawn to a lawn service or hire a licensed service provider to prepare your tax forms. You can buy a dishwasher or maybe use the dishwasher that has been sitting in your kitchen unused for ages.

Some activities in the SPEND category are simply unavoidable. You must use the bathroom (or similar facility) to eliminate waste. You have no choice! Someone in your household has to take out the trash. In theory, you could outsource shopping for food and fuel to personal shopping assistants or even online grocery shopping which was very popular during COVID. In reality, most people shop for their own food and fuel.

One of the most challenging SPEND time situations many of us encounter is dealing with a medical situation.

Undergoing chemotherapy is obviously not enjoyable and may result in harm if someone who "needed" it didn't do it. Such significant medical situations may be considered SPEND time, but some people have found ways to convert at least some of the SPEND time into INVEST time by creating value for themselves and society that is fulfilling. An outstanding example is the inspirational beautiful music created by Nightbirde after being diagnosed with cancer and a 2% chance of survival. This heroic conversion of SPEND time into INVEST time will be described in Chapter 11.

On a much lower intensity issue, I had a triple fracture in two bones in my ankle after a nasty fall a year ago. I was using the app "**Be Happier**" when this occurred and I continued using the app "**Be Happier**" during my months of recovery after surgery. In the first few weeks, my home screen was yellow as I was SPENDING time during the recovery since it was hard to mentally focus on enjoyable and fulfilling work at home. In other words, I was not enjoying my time and it would cause harm if I didn't do it (e.g., removing the uncomfortable cast was not feasible). However, once I was able to concentrate even a little bit, I started talking with family and friends and I would tap the green INVEST button on the app "**Be Happier**." When I did that, I was able to see my Happiness Score increase on the app's home screen and that feedback from the app actually made me feel better. Three months after the injury, I started physical therapy to stand and then walk. The physical therapist was excellent and I definitely tapped the green INVEST button in the app "**Be Happier**" during physical therapy, which increased my Happiness Score. Within a few months, I returned to walking with my wife for 70 minutes every day on a trail through the forest near our house. That is all INVEST time even though full recovery from my injury is still projected to be a few months away as of this initial writing. Eight months after the injury, I walked 120,000 steps in one week while on vacation. My health obviously improved and my Happiness Score improved.

The point is that there are different medical situations of various severities and challenges. While we may not have much choice but to SPEND time recovering, we still might have enough choice that, with a little creativity, we can figure out ways to INVEST time during a period of life that may be dominated by coping with the medical challenges. If you are able, please make every creative attempt possible to figure out ways to INVEST time, even during challenging SPEND time situations.

SPEND - Summary of Key Points

- SPEND time is time during which you are engaged in activity that you don't enjoy but would result in harm if you didn't do it.

- SPEND time activities are often the lowest hanging fruit for increasing your Happiness Score by converting SPEND time into INVEST time, often with little to no resources.

- Name your SPEND time activities in the app "**Be Happier.**"

- Make a **written** list of SPEND time activities. This is your biggest opportunity list to **BE HAPPIER** for most people.

- The #1 or #2 source of SPEND time in the lives of many millions of people occurs because they don't enjoy their occupation or workplace; the Happiness Score will NEVER exceed 67 as long as you do not enjoy your occupation and/or workplace. Read and study Chapter 13 ("Happiness at Work") for details.

CHAPTER 9

WASTE Time

We defined WASTE time as time during which you are "**engaged in an activity that causes harm to you or others**."

Remember that if you are causing harm and enjoying the activity, this is still defined as WASTE time (such as getting high using illegal drugs or gaming so many hours that you don't satisfy responsibilities for family, work or sleep).

WASTE TIME ACTIVITIES LIST

(Examples of activities that cause harm to you or others)

Add and delete activities on this list to create YOUR OWN WASTE TIME LIST

- Yelling at family members
- Bullying, including cyber
- Acting violently (physically or verbally)
- Being a victim of repeated violence (physical or verbal)
- Breaking the law
- Driving aggressively, road rage
- Using illegal drugs or getting drunk
- Self-sabotage (at work, at home, in finances)
- Add your own: _____
- Add your own: _____

The list of WASTE time activities should be much shorter than the activity lists for INVEST and SPEND. Nevertheless, we need to be aware of every instance of WASTE time because they have a disproportionately high negative impact on your Happiness Score. Please make a list of activities that you do, even occasionally, that cause harm or result in harm to yourself and/or others.

Provided it is safe for you to do so, write down a potential solution for every item on your WASTE time list. If you are in a high-risk situation such as spousal abuse or relationships with other extremely toxic or harmful people, you may need to take special safety precautions if you feel it is dangerous for you to even write down your list of WASTE time activities.

Always **keep safety as a paramount consideration** when you write down potential solutions to high-risk situations. Be open to the possibility that you may need the help of licensed professionals in order to resolve, eliminate or mitigate WASTE time events. Your health and safety should always be your top priority so make your decisions very carefully to ensure your safety.

WASTE time activities and events are often the most challenging to resolve and may require careful planning, resources and creativity. Of course, freeing yourself from severe WASTE time activities can be a crucially important step to regain control of your life and your happiness.

For some of you, eliminating your sources of WASTE time, might absolutely be required to first have a better or so-called "normal" life, then later have a happy life. If your situation is so dire, eliminating or reducing your sources of WASTE time might be the most serious and most important thing you ever do in your life. Please seek qualified professionals to help if necessary, so you achieve your goals SAFELY. If you or someone you know is struggling or in crisis, help is available. In the United States, call or text 988 or chat 988lifeline.org (988 Suicide & Crisis Lifeline).

OPPORTUNITY LIST TO REDUCE WASTE TIME

_____
(Fill in your name)

Following are activities that I **CURRENTLY** do that cause harm

_____

_____

_____

_____

_____

WASTE - Summary of Key Points

- WASTE time is time during which you are engaged in activity that causes harm to you and/or others.

- Your Happiness Score goes down dramatically when you WASTE time.

- Make whatever changes necessary in order to SAFELY minimize WASTE time in your life.

- WASTE time is the absolute worst use of time.

- Make sure that the actions you take to minimize WASTE time **can be done safely**! Engage licensed professionals safely if needed!

CHAPTER 10

SLEEP

We defined SLEEP as time during which you are actually asleep or going to sleep.

While there are apps that can detect when you are asleep, we decided to start counting the time of SLEEP when you actually go to sleep. One reason is a practical one and that is that you cannot tap the blue SLEEP button on the app after you have fallen asleep! I personally tap the blue SLEEP button when I turn out the light and lay my head on my pillow without any intended further distractions, including the use of my smartphone.

Sometimes, we have trouble falling asleep or staying asleep. What do we do then?

I am at the age at which I get up an average of twice per night for what engineers in my field call "mass balance." Believe it or not, I actually use the app "**Be Happier**" to manage my behavior when I return to bed.

How?

The temptation when getting back into bed at 2:27 am is to open the phone and check Email or play just one round of Wordle (or whatever game is in vogue at the time). I made a rule for myself that if I open any app on my phone in the middle of the night when I should be sleeping, I must tap the red WASTE button and keep losing points until I go back to sleep, at which time I can truthfully tap the blue SLEEP button. I even tap the Activities tab and name my WASTE time segment "Gaming" or "Internet." It makes me feel self-guilt and motivates me to stop playing as soon as possible, put the darn phone away and tap the blue SLEEP button.

You might think that I am making up this story to prove a point. Well, I'm not.

One of the great characteristics of the app "**Be Happier**" is that it really is personal and no one other than me knows what or when I tap, or why. No one other than me knows what actions I take. I don't need to impress anyone because no one knows (unless I disclose like right now).

I can tell you that once I decide on a disciplined rule in my life, like being a safe driver or tapping on the red WASTE button when I am WASTING time playing a game that is harming me because I don't sleep, the feedback loop really does prevent me (USUALLY!) from engaging in the self-sabotaging behavior of playing video games when I wake up in the middle of the night.

If you have absolutely no self-discipline, you may not be able to extract the most benefit from measuring your Happiness Score and taking corrective action. But if you have just one ounce (or one gram) of discipline in your mind, you will likely be amazed at how you can improve your life, both in the smallest of ways and in major life-changing ways by using the app "**Be Happier**" with all the power with which it was designed, that in turn empowers YOU to take a lot more control of your life and **BE HAPPIER**.

CHAPTER 11

The Most Important Strategic Decisions You Make in Life

"More than half of our performance in life depends on a handful of crucial strategic decisions and less than half of our performance in life depends on our tactical execution. Yet most people dedicate almost all of their time to optimizing the execution of their non-existent strategic plan."

— Marc Halpern

I was lucky to realize the validity of the statement above when I was in my thirties.

By the time I was in my 60s, after I had a chance to observe and coach a lot of people, I wrote: "Most people waste at least 1-2 decades of their lives trying to optimize conquering a hill, only to realize when they reach the top, that it was the wrong hill." Part of the motivation to write this book is to help people stop wasting decades of their lives when it is often avoidable.

These are negative statements and I am usually a positive guy. But these STRATEGIC statements are based on frustrating observations of less-than-happy friends, family and coaching clients that ultimately led me to define the Happiness Score and motivated me to try to help people to **BE HAPPIER**, including by writing this book.

As mentioned several times in earlier chapters, everyone is different and everyone has different activities that they enjoy as well as different circumstances that lead to less-than-optimal happiness over decades of their lives.

At the same time, all it takes is simple observation of the happiest people we know, the unhappiest we know, and everyone else in between, to lead to the obvious conclusion that among all the crucial strategic decisions in life, **there are two special strategic decisions** that most people (though not everyone) make in life that affect happiness for years, decades and sometimes entire lifetimes of adulthood.

Those crucial strategic decisions are:

1. **Choice of relationships, especially life partner**

2. **Choice of primary occupation**

Many people, though certainly not all, make these two crucial strategic decisions in their 20s or early 30s, before they have enough data and life experience to predict all of the ramifications of these two decisions.

It's no wonder then that the divorce rate is high and job satisfaction is so low (supporting data will be presented in Chapters 12 and 13). Many people make these two crucial strategic life decisions without the benefit of underlying supporting information.

Maybe I got lucky when I made these two strategic decisions in my 20s because I have been happily married for 43 years (since age 26) and I still greatly enjoy working in the field phase-transfer catalysis (I ran my first PTC reaction at age 22). Then again, at age 50, I added a new occupation of part-time real estate investing, in order to ensure that I will continue to maintain a Happiness Score above 90 for the rest of my life by avoiding potential financial tension of insufficient income and insufficient net worth in retirement that can get in the way of happiness. Being rich does not cause happiness, but the financial tension of having to choose between food and medicine when the money is not there can cause significant harm, which is WASTE time. In other words, while money cannot buy happiness, avoiding financial tension is crucial to avoid WASTING time.

Remember that WASTE time detracts from the Happiness Score at the highest rate. The simple math in the Happiness Score equation shows that if WASTE time exceeds INVEST time, **the Happiness Score turns negative!**

Look at everyone you know at every stage of adult life and you will realize, even qualitatively, that the happiness of most people in your sphere of influence (though not everyone), is likely affected more by relationship choices and choice of occupation than by any other factors, for both high-happiness and low-happiness individuals. The only exception that is common is health issues, especially those affected by genetics or external factors (COVID-19 for example), that are often not a result of choices made during adult life. Those types of health issues are beyond the scope of this book. Then again, making healthy lifestyle choices, such as diet and exercise, can affect your Happiness Score and they will be addressed later in this book (Chapter 14).

In particular, the two strategic decisions about choosing relationships (especially life partner) and choosing primary occupation are so crucial and so common that chapters will be dedicated to each one of these topics.

An advantage of using the Happiness Score as a tool to **BE HAPPIER** is that you will be able to see tangible progress along the journey, not just when reaching the destination, if you make effective decisions to **BE HAPPIER** without causing harm. This applies with greater impact to choices you make for relationships and occupation.

FIX IT, LIVE WITH IT OR LEAVE IT

In 1989, I was still an employee in corporate America and my employer brought in-house all kinds of management training courses. One of those courses was called "How to Handle Difficult People." I remember one takeaway message of conventional wisdom from that course that is important to share here in case you never heard it before. It is so important that you might want to bookmark or dogear this page for future reference. The message was:

> **In a difficult situation, there are three, and ONLY three, options:**
> 1. **Fix it** *(safely)*
> 2. **Live with it** *(safely)* **OR**
> 3. **Leave it** *(safely)*

Whenever you have stress from a SPEND situation or a WASTE situation, it is usually worthwhile to pause for a moment (only if safe to do so) and perform this analysis calmly and systematically.

How?

First, you ask yourself, "Can I **fix** this problem?" If the answer is no, you then ask yourself "Can I **live with** this problem?" If the answer is still no, you then ask yourself "Can I **leave** this problem?" If the answer to all three questions is no, go back to the beginning and ask the three questions again, in the same order![4]

Why?

The reality is that if you don't (or can't) fix the problem and you don't (or can't) leave the problem, then you will almost certainly continue to live with the problem!

If you continue to live with the problem, this is likely a source of SPEND time or WASTE time and your Happiness Score will remain low until you **fix it** or **leave it**.

Sometimes, the thought process of **fix it**, **live with it** or **leave it** can be applied to temporary situations. I was once sitting with my teenage son on a plane in Newark scheduled to depart at 6:30 pm bound for a major hub in Europe. We were settling in for the long flight. The flight was fully booked and passenger boarding was almost complete. All of a

---

[4] Always make sure that you ask yourself these questions with safety as top priority.

sudden, we felt a small nudge. A few seconds later, the pilot announced that the flight was cancelled and we all had to deplane because a fuel truck hit one of the engines, putting our plane out of service. He said that gate agents would help everyone rebook their flights, including the majority of the passengers who had connecting flights through the hub.

The chaotic next six hours were nothing less than a fascinating study of human behavior under moderate stress. I observed all three options of **fix it**, **live with it** or **leave it** among the people waiting to rebook their flights that night. Irrational decisions were made by some and their outcomes were not optimal. Others chose the non-productive path of complaining which only delayed an ultimate positive outcome. I took advantage of the situation to teach my son how to handle such situations in a rational manner when others were going crazy. In the end, my son and I boarded a flight in another terminal after only 6 hours of delay which was a very good outcome considering the circumstances. On the other hand, one passenger simply left the airport in anger. I chose to **fix it**. The passenger who left obviously decided to **leave it**. Who had a better outcome?

To be fair, sometimes you really can NOT **fix** the problem. One of our friends was having marital problems and she tried to **fix it** by asking her husband to join her in couple's therapy. She discovered that her husband "could not be fixed." By definition, since she couldn't **fix it,** her choices narrowed to the choices of continuing to **live with him** or **leave him**. The final result was that she **lived with him** for 10 more years (while being unhappy for another decade!) before she finally took action to **leave it** (divorce) and put an end to the daily anger and arguing. A decade of irreversible time of her life was wasted.

My father was a teenager when World War II devastated millions of lives in the Western world through atrocities of scope and magnitude most of us cannot begin to comprehend. The Nazis murdered my father's parents (my grandparents), stole their house and store and put my father into slavery in death camps and hard labor camps for 3.5 years with minimal food and no ability to openly own possessions. This was definitely an unimaginably tough situation. **My father didn't have any**

realistically viable options to <u>fix it</u> or <u>leave it!</u> In the end, he **<u>lived with it</u>** until liberated by American soldiers from the hellish conditions. He then proceeded to **<u>fix it</u>** for the rest of his life. He started to **<u>fix it</u>** almost immediately after liberation. Overcome with anger within 24 hours of his liberation, he and some friends (newly freed slaves) burned down a building that was still flying the Nazi flag. Thereafter he dedicated his life to education as a teacher, principal and community leader over the next seven decades (including being married to my mother for 69 years).

Fortunately, most of us do not live in totalitarian North Korea or in pre-1989 East Berlin where people were shot trying to scale the walls to **<u>leave it</u>**. Most of us reading this book live in a free enough society to be able to pursue happiness, even though it is not always easy.

Sometimes the option of **<u>leave it</u>** is possible but requires a huge amount of planning. An example is leaving a physically abusive relationship with a violent spouse after very carefully putting in place adequate safety mechanisms in order to keep the detachment unharmed, such as discreetly recruiting a team of individuals to orchestrate a safe move to a battered women's shelter.

Another example of a major life change to **<u>leave it</u>** is going to night school for a few years to change occupations in order to prevent a few additional decades of working in a job that you hate.

While those are extreme situations, some of you reading this book may very well be in a situation where **<u>leave it</u>** may be the only path to happiness and where massive logistics AND significant risk management may be required. No doubt that these are very tough situations without easy answers. But that doesn't change the fact that **<u>in difficult situations, you have only three choices: fix it (safely), live with it (safely) or leave it (safely)</u>**. You still have a decision to make and if you don't **<u>fix it</u>** or **<u>leave it</u>**, you are effectively choosing to **<u>live with it</u>**, which still might be your best option.

For cases in which safety is an issue, safety may be the dominating factor in your decision to **<u>live with it</u>** (like my father did when he really had no choice), **<u>fix it</u>** (perhaps by calling the police if a burglar enters your home) or **leave it** (such as during an active mass shooting). In extreme situations, always keep in mind that safety is top priority.

If you or someone you know is struggling, is in crisis or even considering suicide, help is available. In the United States, call or text 988 or chat 988lifeline.org (988 Suicide & Crisis Lifeline).

I don't want to go into too many personal details here, but if you read between the lines in my Final Comments at the end of this book, you will see that in my teenage years "I was depressed most of the time, angry the rest of the time and felt worthless all of the time." Consider what a waste it would have been if I was not here to write this book, had I taken certain negative actions based on my feelings of worthlessness as a teenager (Crisis Lifeline was not available back then).

Some of the most excruciating situations involve serious medical problems. Those are also sometimes the most heroic of situations.

An example is the singer Jane Kristen Marczewski, known as "Nightbirde." She was diagnosed with breast cancer at age 16. I first saw her on America's Got Talent and I immediately downloaded her beautiful and emotionally powerful song "It's OK" to my "Best Songs" playlist, to which I listen every day during my 70-minute walk. In the midst of her physical pain, Nightbirde created meaningful musical content for millions of people to enjoy and be inspired. Nightbirde manufactured INVEST time while in pain! This was heroic. Nightbirde famously said, "I have a two percent chance of survival, but two percent is not zero percent. Two percent is something, and I wish people knew how amazing it is."

If you need a moment of inspiration and emotional uplift, I strongly suggest that you listen to Nightbirde's song "It's OK" and consider adding it to your playlist if you have not already done so (shortened version at https://www.youtube.com/watch?v=CZJvBfoHDk0). Nightbirde also famously said, "you can't wait until life isn't hard any more before you decide to be happy." Powerful! Nightbirde died at age 31 in February 2022.

Discussing these difficult situations is very hard, but when we are SPENDING or WASTING large amounts of time in our lives, the clock is ticking. The analysis of **fix it**, **live with it** or **leave it** will usually help you figure out **IF AND HOW** you can (or cannot) make changes that will ultimately enable you to **BE HAPPIER**, and if you can make the change safely without causing harm to yourself or others.

As we move on to the next chapters of this book that will address the choices that we make to convert SPEND time into INVEST time and to convert WASTE time into INVEST time, **always keep in mind that the decisions and actions to minimize activities that we do NOT ENJOY or cause HARM, more often than not require an analysis of your options to fix it, live with it or leave it**.

CHAPTER 12

Happiness in Relationships and Choosing a Life Partner

Humans are social beings and we interact with each other in relationships.

For most people, **relationships with other people are the greatest source of INVEST time.** This is a natural outcome of enjoying the company of family members who we love, friends who we choose and others we meet such as coworkers.

On the flip side, for most people, **relationships with other people are also the greatest source of WASTE time!** This is a natural outcome of hurt, pain and sometimes suffering experienced when relationships go wrong with family, friends, coworkers and others. Moments of yelling, loss of dignity, violence, anger, and bullying are just a few classic examples that fall within the definition of WASTE time.

Relationships are tricky. So tricky, that even though the concepts in this book can help characterize and identify situations in which we INVEST, SPEND or WASTE time, we cannot cover this subject comprehensively. In fact, licensed psychologists, psychiatrists, sociologists, medical professionals and even police may be required to manage relationships in various situations. Do not make any decisions and/or take any action based on the content of this book that may cause harm or loss to yourself or others without first ensuring your safety which may include consulting with relevant qualified licensed professionals.

What we CAN do here is state the obvious which is:

- We want to maximize the time we INVEST in relationships which means enjoying time and activities with other people without causing harm to ourselves or others.

- We want to minimize the time we WASTE in relationships which means time during which we feel or cause pain, fear or harm from interactions with other people.

In particular, continuous monitoring of our Happiness Score using the app "**Be Happier**," can provide each one of us with valuable information to help us recognize how much time we INVEST in enjoyable constructive relationships and how much time we WASTE in destructive harmful relationships.

In this chapter, we will highlight examples of choices we make for happiness in relationships and we will end this chapter with a discussion of the biggest choice most of us make (though not all of us) in our entire lives that affects happiness, which is the choice of life partner.

First let's start with examples of INVEST time, SPEND time and WASTE time in relationships.

RELATIONSHIPS	
INVEST	family quality time (if enjoyable without causing harm), date night, mentoring, visiting friends, reading to kids, bowling league, consensual intimate time, book club, girls' night out
SPEND	meetings with boss
WASTE	disrespectful arguing, verbal abuse, physical abuse, bullying

If you live in a household with other people such as a life partner, children, parents, siblings or even friends (like in the sitcom "Friends"), then there is a very good chance that your Happiness Score is more affected by the relationships in your household than any other factor. Why? Because the Happiness Score is based on the hours you INVEST, SPEND and WASTE. Most people are present in their households for more hours than anywhere else, including work. Don't forget about the weekends.

That means that your relationships in your household are most likely to be the #1 source of your happiness, for good and for bad.

For that reason, it is worthwhile for you to do something that might be awkward or even very uncomfortable and that is to analyze and characterize the hours you INVEST, SPEND and WASTE with each member of your household.

When you understand how much time you are INVESTING, SPENDING and WASTING at home, you can then know if and how you can maximize INVEST time and minimize SPEND time and WASTE time.

If your home life is "good" (good is a qualitative term), then it might not be crucial to analyze the time you INVEST, SPEND and WASTE at home.

But if you feel that your home life is not what it should be, then you may be in a difficult situation in which you have the three choices of **fix it**, **live with it** or **leave it** (safely of course).

If your home life needs improvement, then identifying the specific time segments with specific activities that are SPEND time and especially WASTE time, will help you understand which activities and times need resolution.

On the positive side, tracking the time segments and activities at home that cause joy and fulfillment, will help you understand what choices you can make to increase your INVEST time at home. This can be done extremely easily if you use the free app "**Be Happier**" and you name your activities.

For example, the app "**Be Happier**" can alert you to the opportunity to increase INVEST time by making choices, such as talking with your children at dinner time instead of watching depressing political news shows.

For those of you with young children, you know how relaxing and bond-strengthening it is to read books to your young children as they go to bed. If you name an INVEST time segment in the "Activities" table of the app "**Be Happier**" as "Reading with Kids," then when you review your weekly or monthly data, you might realize how much of a great opportunity you have to increase your Happiness Score by making a conscious effort to read books with your children every night possible.

In fact, for those of you using the app "**Be Happier**," we recommend that you name as many activities (time segment events) as possible since they help you analyze and identify numerous opportunities to increase INVEST time and minimize SPEND time and WASTE time. This is the most important outcome you can achieve by continuously monitoring your Happiness Score and its components. This is the major reason that we created the app "**Be Happier**."

You should create your own list of activity names that are customized to YOUR life. Some examples of names you might use to name your activities (time segment events) of INVEST, SPEND and WASTE in your relationships are shown in the table on the previous page. Add your own as appropriate. The more you name your activities in the app, the better you will understand where you are now (your current Happiness Score) and what changes you will want to make to increase your Happiness Score and **BE HAPPIER**.

When we do not track our Happiness Score and we do not name activities in the app as INVEST, SPEND or WASTE, we run the risk of not consciously recognizing shifts or slow drifts in relationships. Following are some examples.

Some relationships with friends or intimate partners start out nearly exclusively as blissful INVEST time segments, then shift (slowly or rapidly) into more WASTE time, which in extreme cases can deteriorate into nearly exclusively painful and toxic WASTE time. Some marriages evolve in that way and it is extremely important to recognize when and if the relationship transitions into being toxic, especially if it is gradual. If you are monitoring the time you INVEST, SPEND and WASTE with that person, you will be able to detect the destructive change earlier because your Happiness Score will tip you off. Relationships can be tricky and you must be consciously aware of the snapshot status of your key relationships at every moment.

When such a shift from INVEST to WASTE starts to occur in a relationship, most of us tend to make excuses to justify ignoring the first signs of change in observed behavior of the friend or partner. Eventually, we usually realize that something is wrong and we are WASTING time with that person. The next actions you take for damage control depend on how far the relationship has deteriorated and how the other person is expected to react to attempts at resolution or detachment. Again, ensuring safety is a paramount consideration when contemplating changes to a harmful or toxic relationship and professional counseling may be required so it can be done safely. You may need to consider safety when recording your activities in the app or in writing.

Sometimes we get used to destructive harmful relationships that WASTE valuable irreversible time while the clock continues to tick during the remainder of our lives. That is a shame. The Happiness Score can alert us to the need for change to resolve the relationships that WASTE valuable time.

Another more common example of a relationship that may be tricky to navigate, is when your interactions with another person can be enjoyable INVEST time at some times and harmful or painful WASTE time at other times. This requires you to effectively manage the relationship with that person in order to maximize INVEST time and minimize WASTE time. Again, progress toward resolution may be as simple as open communication or may be as complicated as involving professional counseling assistance.

In some relationships, you may **perceive** that you need the other person to protect you from harm even though you don't enjoy the interaction with the other person. In that case, you may perceive that you are SPENDING time with that person. You need to be cautious with that perception because there may be manipulation going on. Such manipulation of relationships can occur at home or at work[5] or in other settings.

The last few paragraphs highlighted negative developments in relationships. Let's not lose perspective by fearing that most relationships turn into bad news. There is a lot of good news when it comes to relationships and the good news is that we have choices.

---

[5] I once worked in a postdoctoral position for a professor in a university who convinced his graduate students and other "postdoc's" that they couldn't get a job without his recommendation. The graduate students and postdoc's mostly did not enjoy their interactions with the professor but felt they had no choice. Some continued to work extra unhappy years with that professor because they perceived that if they didn't, it would cause them harm. Under their perception, this was SPEND time because if they left without the recommendation and the graduate degree, it would cause harm of being unemployable. I saw what was going on and I started interviewing for jobs without the professor's knowledge. I chose to **leave it**. I accepted a good job with a good company and when I notified the professor that I would be leaving, he immediately insisted that he write a recommendation letter to my new boss to protect his power base. I responded that it was not necessary since I was offered and accepted the job **without his recommendation**. I left the postdoc position after only 8 months of a planned 2-year term. When the other graduate students and postdoc's saw that I actually got a job without the professor's recommendation, several of them started interviewing and left, one of whom worked for 6 years including two years of menial work beyond his valuable research. Sometimes the perception of harm by ending a relationship is valid and real. Sometimes, it is just a manipulation. You must determine how much if any harm will happen to you if you are able to safely disconnect from the relationship.

GOOD NEWS FOR MANY RELATIONSHIPS — WE CAN MAKE CHOICES

The good news is that as we mature into adulthood, we can choose with whom and how to interact with others. **The ability to make choices in relationships gives us the greatest opportunity to control, or at least influence, our Happiness Score**.

Most relationships result from choices we make, such as choosing friends. Some relationships are forced upon us from birth.

It turns out that once we become adults, we have a lot of choices, and even control, with whom we interact and have relationships.

It is said that you can't choose family. Maybe so, but you can often choose what kind of relationship you have with each individual family member. The unspoken reality sometimes is that you might be closer to one parent than another. You might be closer to one sibling than another. You might have more of a loving relationship and/or cooperative relationship with one family member or another. You might be engaged in an abusive relationship with one family or another.

Once you become an adult, you have a lot more choice and control over relationships with family members, even when you didn't choose them at the outset like you could with friends.

It is very powerful to realize that, in most cases, you can ESTABLISH ACCEPTABLE STANDARDS OF BEHAVIOR with others. This is particularly valid for friends since you get to choose your friends from the outset through a go/no-go decision that YOU make.

It is also common sense to realize that good relationships grow organically as long as they remain good. When you are enjoying a relationship with a person that is not harmful, you are INVESTING time with that person and you naturally gravitate toward INVESTING more time with that person.

In contrast, when you are experiencing harm or fear in a relationship with a person, you are WASTING time with that person. In such a case, you naturally gravitate AWAY from WASTING more time with that person, but fear may keep you longer in the relationship than is good for you. In those situations, safety should be a dominant factor in making decisions about proceeding forward. Consultation with licensed professionals is likely an advantageous path if it can be done safely.

> **It is very powerful when you realize that in most cases, you can ESTABLISH ACCEPTABLE STANDARDS OF BEHAVIOR in your interactions with others.**

Let's get back to the positive phenomenon of INVESTING time. The driving force for INVESTING more time with that person may lead to a very strong relationship or even a status change to life partner. As long as the time is enjoyable and without harm, the relationship can thrive until death do you part. I'm quite confident that the 43 years of marriage with my wife is such a relationship.

CHOOSING A LIFE PARTNER

Ultimately, most people (though not all) choose one special person to be a life partner or at least that's the intention when the relationship is taken to that level.[6] Pew Research Center analysis of census data found that in 2019, 38% of adults ages 25 to 54 were unpartnered – that is, neither married nor living with a partner.[7]

---

[6] Some people can **BE HAPPIER** without a life partner. If that is your situation, do not regard this portion of the chapter as pressure to conform to societal norms. Every person is different and has different needs and wants. As long as a person can **BE HAPPIER** without causing harm to themselves or others, lifestyle choices should be an individual right.

[7] https://www.pewresearch.org/social-trends/2021/10/05/rising-share-of-u-s-adults-are-living-without-a-spouse-or-partner/#fn-31655-1

I am not an expert in life partnerships, but common sense can be applied to figure out a few basic thoughts that should be considered when entering into a life partnership.

First and most obvious, in a good life partnership, the two partners should enjoy each other's company without causing harm. This is the definition of INVEST time and it certainly applies here.

If you are with your partner and if you have the app "**Be Happier**" running passively in the background on your smartphone, your home screen should be in the green INVEST zone. If you are not enjoying the time with your partner (SPEND) or if you are feeling fear or pain in their presence (WASTE), something is the matter in the relationship at that moment. What are your options in a difficult situation? **Fix it**, **live with it** or **leave it** (safely of course).

The most common way to attempt to **fix it** is by communicating. This is why open communication to discuss differences of viewpoints or problems, then resolve them, is one of the most important factors in a successful relationship. This is just common sense.

Open communication prevents differences of viewpoint from evolving into problems. **The earlier the communication the better**!

Following is an example of how one single event of communication changed the rest of my life. My parents were married for 69 years when my father passed away. They loved each other and did great things together. But they did argue a lot. I grew up thinking that frequent arguments were normal. In fact, most people grow up in households in which arguments with raised voices are common. When my wife was a young girl, she decided she did not want to raise her voice during a disagreement. About a month before our wedding day, I had a difference of opinion with my wife-to-be and I raised my voice in protest over the issue at hand. My wife-to-be immediately and firmly responded (without raising her voice) that raising my voice is unacceptable behavior when we have a difference of opinion. She actually gave me an ultimatum. I had to decide right then and there if I was going to change my normal behavior for addressing differences of opinion without raising my voice or finding another spouse! My wife-to-be was establishing the acceptable standard of behavior discussed earlier. What do you think happened?

It turns out that was the last ultimatum she ever presented and I changed my behavior. After that single pre-marital dispute, in our first 30 years of marriage, I raised my voice five times (I know…I counted…each one was unusual and not pleasant afterwards!). That averaged once every six years. In contrast, my parents averaged raising their voice once per day! I have not raised my voice in disagreement with my wife since 2010 (going on 14 years now)! Either I am statistically overdue to explode (likely not) or I finally figured out that life is more enjoyable when we communicate openly without raised voices to avoid problems that would otherwise evolve from small differences of opinion.

By the way, to this day I never heard my wife raise her voice, EVER, not even when the kids were growing up. I really lucked out with her.

When you ask people to list their secrets for a successful life partnership, there are a bunch of usual answers like love, communication, respect, intimacy, forgiveness and others. I'm guessing that it varies from couple to couple. But I also know that love does NOT conquer ALL. A factor that is more important than love, is compatibility.

Compatibility matters.

Compatibility of core values is particularly important. Do not confuse core values compatibility with common interests or backgrounds. Anecdotally, my wife and I share identical core values but we shared surprisingly few common interests when we first met. We come from families that speak different languages and are from different cultures. The cement of our relationship, and of many relationships in our sphere of influence, is core values, reinforced by open communication.

I would like to suggest a commonsense activity that most couples do not do before deciding to commit to a life partnership. I would like to suggest doing a COMPATIBILITY ANALYSIS. I know what you're saying, "Marc Halpern is a scientist and he wants to analyze everything!" Well, that's true, but that still does not detract from the value of SPENDING (or INVESTING) some time performing this compatibility analysis early in a relationship.

Notice that I used the word SPEND for engaging in the compatibility analysis. Why? Because it might not be enjoyable to have this conversation, but if you don't do it, it could potentially cause harm in terms of years of unhappiness down the road. That meets our definition of SPEND.

In the compatibility analysis, I suggest purposely discussing key partnership issues such as sharing core values, equality, plans for children including how to raise and educate them, attitude toward INVESTING, SPENDING and WASTING money, intimacy compatibility and other issues that are important to EACH OF YOU, especially issues that may be "deal breakers."

The National Fatherhood Initiative published an excellent study in 2005 entitled "A National Survey On Marriage In America." [8] As unpleasant as it may be to discuss, you may want to consider SPENDING time reviewing the following list of the top 12 reasons for divorce BEFORE deciding to commit to a life partner. Again, the word SPEND is used here because it might not be enjoyable to have this conversation, but if you don't talk through these 12 items, it could potentially cause harm in terms of years or decades of unhappiness down the road. Do you think you should SPEND time discussing these 12 items before getting married or would you rather avoid this discussion and take your chances? That was a rhetorical question.

The 12 items are, in order of frequency cited by divorced partners:

1. Lack of Commitment
2. Too Much Conflict and Arguing
3. Infidelity
4. Married Too Young

---

[8] http://www.healthymarriageinfo.org/wp-content/uploads/2018/05/nms.pdf

5. Unrealistic Expectations
6. Lack of Equality
7. Inadequate Preparation
8. Domestic Violence
9. Financial Problems
10. Conflict about Domestic Work
11. Lack of Family Support
12. Religious Differences

The good news is that there are MANY stable life partnerships. So do not enter every relationship with a fatalistic attitude even if you have seen a lot of breakups around you. Also keep in mind that **if you don't like the choices your partner makes, remember that <u>you were one of their choices</u>**.

One characteristic of some long-term life partnerships is independence or codependence (the opposite of independence). Codependency is when one partner feels an excessive emotional reliance on their partner. I am not an expert and I have not conducted scientific studies, so my observations are only anecdotal. While independence and codependency may be affected by many factors, I speculate but do not know for sure, that a measure of independence may be more desirable than codependency, especially if a long-term life partnership ends in the death of one of the partners. You can imagine that the loss of a partner can be particularly devastating when one partner is extremely codependent on the other and grief may be inconsolable.

My wife and I love each other and we are enjoying a long-life partnership of 43 years so far. At the same time, we both support each other's independent activities of self-actualization. While we share all core values and many current interests (e.g., quality family time, travel), we also respect each other's areas of interest. My wife has three Masters degrees in areas of literature and special education. I have no interest whatsoever in classical literature. I love organic chemistry. My wife has no clue what the difference between methane and ethane is. My wife is an active member of two book clubs. I rarely have the patience to read an entire book to completion (I tend to extract the value from selected portions of the book content). I attend chemical technology tradeshows. I have to go alone for a couple of days because my wife has no interest in my enjoyable field of expertise.

The point is that while we certainly enjoy our time together, trust each other completely and we treat each other with respect all the time, we also engage in independent activities. We are not overly codependent. I think this strengthens our marriage. Others might see things differently.

Let's get back to the big picture. Millions of pages have been written over centuries about successful life partnerships, successful friendships and every type of relationship between people. All of that historical information can't possibly be summarized here.

However, we can certainly apply **common sense** when analyzing INVEST time, SPEND time and WASTE time for our most important relationships.

Note: The following summary statements are nothing more than common sense and are presented here as a basis for organizing your thoughts if your relationships are not as much in the INVEST time category as you would like.

HAPPINESS IN RELATIONSHIPS - Summary of Key Points

- If you are INVESTING time with another person, such as a life partner, family member, friend or other person, you will naturally want to INVEST **MORE** time with that person as long as you continue to enjoy the interaction without causing or experiencing harm.

- If you are WASTING time with another person, such as a life partner, family member, friend or other person, you will naturally want to WASTE **LESS** time with that person as long as you continue to experience or cause harm, fear or pain.

- While it might be unpleasant to deal with a harmful relationship, the cold reality is usually that you have only three options: **fix it**,

live with it or **leave it**. Whatever you choose to do, safety should be a paramount consideration. If safety is an issue, you should manage risk carefully. If safe to do so, consider getting help from appropriate licensed professionals including but not limited to psychologists, social workers, therapists, other mental health workers, possibly police and others.

- If you are contemplating entering into a life partnership, strongly consider INVESTING time (or SPENDING time if unpleasant) jointly analyzing your compatibility for all life components that are important to EACH of you.

- Open communication is often the most effective action to prevent conflict in relationships and minimizes WASTE time and SPEND time, when it can be done safely and without harm. This activity of open communication that prevents escalation into conflict is preferably continuous throughout your lifetime as long as it is safe (causes no harm).

- Monitor the relationship components of your Happiness Score to verify that your relationships are on track or to identify a potential negative drift away from INVESTING time. If and when WASTE time or SPEND time is detected, strongly consider the options of **fix it**, **live with it** or **leave it** as soon as practical and safe after WASTE or SPEND are detected.

- The app "**Be Happier**" is an effective tool for tracking your Happiness Score. If safe to do so (does your partner have access to your smartphone?), when you name Activities of INVEST time, SPEND time and WASTE time, you can more easily identify which relationships are good and which may be starting to drift from INVEST to SPEND or WASTE.

- The clock is ticking. Relationships are CRUCIAL for you to **BE HAPPIER**.

CHAPTER 13

Happiness at Work

The MOST IMPORTANT strategic decision that many people (though not all) make in their lives that affects happiness is **choice of occupation** (and workplace). This is usually true for the 38% of adults who do not choose a life partner. For the other 62%, choice of occupation (and workplace) is usually the second most important strategic decision in life that affects happiness, after choosing a life partner.

In other words, if you want to **BE HAPPIER**, choice of occupation is super important.

Let's calculate the MASSIVE impact of choice of occupation on happiness.

If you work 40 hours per week for 48 weeks per year (4 weeks of vacation per year) from age 25 to age 65, that comes out to **76,800 hours** of work time or 4.6 million minutes! That IS massive.

Who determines if you SPEND or INVEST these tens of thousands of hours of your life at work?! That's right, **YOU DO!** It's **YOUR** choice and **YOUR** responsibility!

Who determines if you SPEND or INVEST tens of thousands of hours of your life at work?

YOU DO!
It's **YOUR** choice and **YOUR** responsibility!

If you love what you do to make a living, congratulations!

If you don't enjoy your work, the question is, "Are you willing to compromise tens of thousands of hours over the rest of your life without being happy at work?" That would be a real shame! The good news is that you CAN take action now to **BE HAPPIER**! This chapter will offer suggestions to consider.

As a reminder, INVEST time at work means that you enjoy your work without causing harm. SPEND time at work means that you do NOT enjoy your work but if you didn't do it, you wouldn't have money for food and other basic needs. **Are you SPENDING time at work or INVESTING time? This is one of the most important questions of your entire life!**

If you don't enjoy your work, the reason probably has to do with when you first decided what occupation you would choose. Were you in your late teens or twenties? How much time did you invest in figuring out that decision?

When you were in your late teens or twenties, did you choose your occupation after performing 100 hours of due diligence, collecting relevant data about income, probability of finding a job and the cost of educational prerequisites? Did you assess how much joy and fulfillment you would enjoy from the essence of the work?

Probably not.

Did you even invest 5 hours of analysis that would affect tens of thousands of hours of your happiness?!

Some people do indeed perform a comprehensive analysis of their occupational options in their teens or twenties, but most don't. Many people at that age invest more time figuring out what movie they want to see that evening.

Some teens and twenty-somethings choose their occupation as a "temporary" convenient choice and then get stuck there for years.

Without enough life experience, many teens unsurprisingly postpone this life decision until they go to college. Unfortunately, the college path often costs a whopping $30,000 to $50,000 per year (!) to figure out which field might be the right one. To make matters worse, many students then wind up choosing their college major based on some random factor such as whether they happened to like a certain class or professor.[9]

By the way, you can save tens of thousands of dollars in the US by going to community college for the first year or two and taking a wide variety of courses until you figure out which occupation is likely best for you. That is exactly what my younger son did. In his first year at the local county college, he took courses in business management, photography, religion, physics, education, journalism and art appreciation. I paid a total of only $2,000 per year for my son's self-discovery expedition before he went to a much more expensive college.[10]

Regardless of how, why or at what age you chose your occupation, if you enjoy your occupation (like I do), you hit a happiness jackpot!

If you do NOT enjoy your occupation, the brutal reality is that it is **incomprehensible that you would purposely CHOOSE to SPEND**

---

[9] I attended orientation for new students at Temple University when my son went there and the speaker announced to the audience of more than 1,000 people that the most common major was "undecided!" Imagine paying $30,000 per year without knowing where you're headed! There are more than 10 million full-time college students in the US and more than 6 million part-time students. I bet that more part-time students know what they want to do.

[10] Your college-bound kids are probably not required to follow the recommendations of the community college intake counselor. When my son showed up to choose courses for the first semester, they recommended English Composition, History, Computer Literacy and Accounting. I told him to ignore that boring list and browse the entire list of college courses. The best parenting advice I ever gave him was to choose whatever he thought would be interesting. That was a crucial decision. He already knew he didn't like history from high school. Computer literacy was a waste of time for a teenager. Taking a course in composition would not help him figure out his future profession. He has no interest in accounting. He wound up taking a highly diverse set of inexpensive courses and found himself while enjoying himself in school for the first time!

76,800 hours of your life which might feel like 4.6 million individual minutes!

The good news is, no matter your age, if you currently don't enjoy your work, you can change your occupation or at least change your workplace that would make a major impact on your happiness for the rest of your life. It might take some major effort, but it can be done.

Let's say that you're 45 years old and you have not been enjoying your work for 20 years, which is nearly a whopping 40,000 hours of SPEND time (SO FAR!). Are you willing to give up on enjoying the next 40,000 hours of work?!

If you don't enjoy your current occupation or workplace, you have several options to improve your life, increase your Happiness Score and **BE HAPPIER**. These options will be discussed below.

If you do NOT enjoy your occupation, the brutal reality is that it is incomprehensible that you would purposely CHOOSE to SPEND 76,800 hours of your life!

First, you must recognize that making changes at work will most likely require you to INVEST resources, which consist of time, money, discipline and risk management.

The reason you need to manage risk well is that you need to make sure that your financial needs are covered during the transition period from one occupation or workplace to another, including your family's financial needs, if relevant. Your continued financial viability during your transition from one job/workplace to another or from one occupation to another is usually achievable by maintaining your existing job while preparing for your new job or new occupation. Quitting your current job cold turkey without a financial cushion for the interim is usually not a good path to make the transition. Consult with your professional and/or licensed advisors before you make such decisions or take action to make sure that you will be financially viable during the transition.

The first question to consider is if you like your current occupation but just don't like your current workplace. For example, if you like your current occupation but just don't like your current bad boss, you likely do not need to change occupation, you just may need to find a new employer. How? You "fire your boss," preferably in a diplomatic manner without burning bridges.

If you are not enjoying your work because you don't enjoy the essence of your work, you may need to consider retraining for a new occupation.

That might not be as scary as you think. For example, if you have a job with income and you live in the United States, you can learn to be a part-time real estate investor, using "other people's money" (OPM) from a bank or private lenders. I have a program to teach people with full-time jobs how to be successful part-time real estate investors (www.PartTimeInvestors.com). I started part-time real estate investing as a side business at age 50 to attempt to ensure that we avoid financial tension in retirement (while enjoying my primary occupation). I achieved financial freedom in 11 years by doing only 1-2 real estate deals per year. I kept my primary occupation in chemical technology development (www.PhaseTransferCatalysis.com) during the entire transition and I still engage in both PTC technology and part-time real estate investing. The point is that it CAN be done in reality as an option if you want to change your occupation! This will be discussed later in the section on "Stepping-Stone Occupation."

I am not saying that part-time real estate investing is the optimal path, or even a practical path, for most people. I am suggesting that a carefully chosen side hustle together with appropriate risk management, can be explored as a potential stepping-stone to pursue an occupation that you would enjoy.

The second question that is crucial to **BE HAPPIER** when you don't enjoy your current occupation is to determine what type of occupation you WOULD enjoy. We have a series of exercises that you can perform to identify the types of occupations you may enjoy. These exercises, called the "Personal Occupation Analysis," are available for sale on our website www.NowBeHappier.com. The concept behind the approach to identifying a more suitable occupation, customized especially for you, is based on analyzing and ranking your personal strengths and characteristics along with the activities you enjoy. You can then combine your highest-ranking results to custom design an occupation or business that builds upon your individual strengths, joys and activities that result in personal fulfillment.

Now let's take a deeper look at job satisfaction by considering data from studies. **If you are among the people who are less than happy at work, the data show that you are definitely not alone**.

A wide variety of job satisfaction surveys around the world are funded by large employers. Why? Because employers benefit from lower costs (i.e., higher profits) when employee turnover is minimized. Job satisfaction is a key component of employee retention. So, the corporate motivation to understand job satisfaction is economic and the results of these corporate studies show that most people are not exactly happy at work.

Depending on the survey, the industry, the occupation, the country and other factors, anywhere between 14% and 33% of employees are reported to **LOVE** their jobs (I'm part of that group since I love the thrill of achieving scientific breakthroughs in my primary occupation in R&D). At the other end of the scale, similar numbers of employees actually **HATE** their jobs.

Using another metric of job satisfaction, about half of all employees over the past two decades, "**are not engaged at work**" which means that they feel no real connection to their jobs and tend to do the bare minimum.

Are you part of that half? If so, you should consider making a change to prevent tens of thousands of hours of non-enjoyment going forward!

On top of that, the COVID-19 pandemic brought about "The Great Resignation." Gallup's global workplace report for 2022 showed that only 9% of workers in the UK were engaged or enthusiastic about their work.[11] Wow, by that measure, many millions of people are not happy at work!

If you are not happy at work and you use the app "**Be Happier**," the reality of your low Happiness Score will stare you in the face every day, reminding you that **you will never even achieve a score of 67 until you make a change in your work life**. The use of the app "**Be Happier**" for work is very simple. You tap on the yellow SPEND button when you arrive at work if you don't enjoy your work, then click on the green INVEST button when you arrive home if you enjoy your home life.

Obviously, not everyone has an undesirable occupation. For example, one survey of 86 professions found that 98% of clergy feel that they have a meaningful job while only 5% of parking lot attendants feel that they have a meaningful job.

All this information puts into perspective a crucial truth about life that you already know, which is that your occupation and workplace are of very high importance to your happiness. If you are not happy at work, the following are several options for your consideration to explore.

OPTION 1: CHANGE YOUR BOSS

If you enjoy the essence of your work but don't like your specific work environment, you may not need to take the drastic course of action to change your occupation.

As mentioned in Chapter 5, many organizations cannot keep up with training so many bosses to be good managers. Not everyone they choose to be a boss is management material or even trainable. Some of you are snickering right now thinking about your incompetent boss.

---

[11] https://www.gallup.com/workplace/349484/state-of-the-global-workplace-2022-report.aspx

If your problem is <u>your boss and NOT your occupation</u>, then one of your options may include asking to be transferred to another department or another location in the organization if your company is big enough.

Again, you must carefully plan how to ask for the transfer without causing harm to your career at the company if you choose to stay there for many more years. Some large companies have an "employee assistance program" that allows stressed employees to confidentially ask professional counselors about options to reduce stress. Smart companies invest in such an assistance department because stressed employees are less productive. Retaining good employees is less expensive than replacing them.

If your company does not have options internally for a lateral move or a promotion in your current occupation, you can consider very carefully and discreetly inquiring about opportunities outside of your employer. Again, be sure to implement good risk management practices before taking any action.

You may be afraid of the risk of making such inquiries or the amount of time and effort required to look for another job, which might not even result in a good outcome. In fact, the risk and large amount of effort may be outside of your normal comfort zone.

While these are valid thoughts, **consider the tens of thousands of hours of non-enjoyable work you will begrudgingly perform day after day, week after week, month after month, year after year, decade after decade if you simply accept to live with your current situation**. Is that acceptable? What's riskier, to remain in an unfulfilling job or to at least make some inquiries (if they can be done safely without causing you harm)?

I had four jobs in my field of chemical technology breakthrough R&D before I set out on my own as a full-time small business entrepreneur. I loved the essence of my occupation in R&D. I loved two of my R&D jobs while two I didn't like, mostly because of the boss. The first job I didn't like was totally due to the surprising incompetence of the boss (who was a leader in the field). I took action rather quickly and my total time at that job was 8 months from hiring to leaving. The second job I didn't like was due to my boss's boss and organizational plans that were not compatible with mine. I left only 15 months after being hired and they even offered me a double promotion to stay. Instead, I got a quadruple promotion to Director of R&D at another company and doubled my salary at the same time.

Did these transitions require effort? Yes. But the stress of working for a bad boss and/or an incompatible organization was not worth the stress and non-happiness for many future years of my life that is not reversible.

Can you identify with this thought process? Are you stuck with a bad boss? Would you like to feel that you are not only of value but an integral part of a "mission" or something larger than yourself that creates a synergy and pride in what you do?

If you are not happy at work and if you are hesitant to take any action to **BE HAPPIER**, please go back and now read the **FIX IT, LIVE WITH IT, LEAVE IT** section of Chapter 11. Are you REALLY willing to **live with it**?!

Your answer will affect about 2,000 hours of your happiness each year in your future irreversible life.

OPTION 2: CHANGE OCCUPATION

Changing occupation mid-career or choosing your first occupation (if you are a college student for example) is definitely a MAJOR life change that will impact your Happiness Score ENORMOUSLY, likely for the rest of your working life! Such a decision is not trivial and involves significant investment of resources, especially time and money. Planning and execution of significant logistics will be required, especially if the person changing occupation is the primary breadwinner for a family that has routine household expenses to meet basic needs for food, shelter, clothing, etc.

You may perceive that the decision to change to a new occupation mid-career might come down to a choice or compromise between your personal happiness and the need to meet basic household expenses.

Let's talk about that.

The first factor to consider doesn't require any money and can require INVESTING anywhere between 5 minutes and 5 hours of your time and is identifying an occupation that will bring you joy and fulfillment from the essence of the work itself. For example, recall the citation above for job satisfaction of clergy versus parking attendant.

If you already know which occupation you would enjoy, then you can proceed to analyze the income potential and stability of that occupation to determine if it will enable you to meet the routine expenses of your household.

If you don't already know which occupation will bring you joy and fulfillment, we have created a program that helps people identify potential occupations that are customized to their specific situations. The process of this program is described below. Again, you can purchase the "Personal Occupation Analysis" program on our website www.NowBeHappier.com.

In principle, the program starts by **writing** lists that include a list of all of the activities you enjoy, your strengths and your personal characteristics. Personal characteristics include "soft" non-quantifiable personal characteristics such as integrity and tangible items such as the county in which you live.

The list of activities that you enjoy is then ranked with the top 5-10 rising to the top of the list. People typically INVEST 15-60 minutes to create and rank this list. This is usually a fun and uplifting activity which is why it is categorized as INVEST time.

You then rank your list of strengths and positive personal characteristics with the top 10 or more rising to the top of the list. People typically INVEST an hour or more to create and rank this list. This activity is also usually a fun and uplifting activity which is why it too is categorized as INVEST time.

Sometimes people who are very humble in their own minds need help with this exercise. They will be well-served to recruit people they trust to add to their list of strengths and positive personal characteristics. For example, someone might point out that you are exceptionally reliable and dependable and you may perceive that to be a standard expectation of everyone and not anything very special. However, a trusted friend who knows you well and has a positive attitude may help you see your real value.

The next step is a "divergent brainstorming session" in which you come up with various combinations (some almost random) of activities you enjoy, your strengths, talents and other positive personal characteristics. In a fun and creative exercise, you (and your "team") start to come up with hypothetical or real occupations that would benefit from each specific combination of activities, strengths, talents and personal characteristics. During divergent brainstorming, you must not eliminate unrealistic occupations or occupations that don't exist. In other words, divergent brainstorming is a "free-for-all" brain exercise without limitation or judgment.

I have conducted many of these sessions with people at various career stages. This "free-thought" brainstorming session often inspires the most amazing creative hypothetical occupations that later turn out to be practical despite initial skepticism.

The next stage is "convergent brainstorming" in which each identified occupation is analyzed IN WRITING for advantages and disadvantages, including factors such as income level and growth potential.

Again, we have created the systematic "Personal Occupation Analysis" that is available for purchase at www.NowBeHappier.com.

To state the obvious, changing occupation may involve significant retraining. That retraining may involve very significant resources, especially time, money and perseverance with mental fortitude. This decision should never be taken lightly.

I have seen salespeople who work at large companies INVEST several years getting their MBA (Masters in Business Administration) while they continue to work at their employer. When they get their degree, they change their occupation for a better job that is more enjoyable and with higher pay. Interestingly enough, the better job may even be at the same company where they worked while going to school.

The point is that changing your occupation is a major strategic decision in life that will likely come at a cost. You will need to make **written** lists ("if it ain't writ, it ain't thunk") to analyze the pros, cons, tradeoffs and potential outcomes of taking action to change your occupation versus the pros, cons, tradeoffs and potential outcomes of **<u>NOT</u>** taking action to change your occupation. Performing this Personal Occupation Analysis will likely require you to INVEST several hours of your time. If that makes you feel uncomfortable, compare that discomfort with the tens of thousands of hours of SPENDING time at work that you don't enjoy.

It's YOUR choice. It's YOUR responsibility. **IT'S <u>YOUR</u> LIFE!!!** Do you want to **BE HAPPIER**?

OPTION 3: ADD A "STEPPING-STONE OCCUPATION"

Full disclosure: I have a bias in favor of adding a "stepping-stone occupation." I will explain the underlying reasoning and assumptions to support my bias so you can judge for yourself whether to accept, reject or partially adopt the strategy of adding a stepping-stone occupation. Just be aware that it is hard for me to separate my bias when writing this section so you must be vigilant and critical about any statement I make in this section, in particular if it doesn't feel right to you.

The main purpose of raising the possibility of adding a stepping-stone occupation in this book is to provide hope to some of you, who are SPENDING your time at work, or possibly even hate your job. A less important purpose of raising this possibility is to give hope to anyone who is struggling financially and sees no way of emerging from the financial tension. However, this book is about happiness and not money, so we will focus on improving happiness.

I define a "stepping-stone occupation" as an occupation that you are likely to enjoy to at least some extent that will serve as an intermediate step toward eventually engaging in an occupation about which you are likely to be passionate. The stepping-stone occupation can be designed to be temporary and most often is initially performed as a side hustle in parallel with your current occupation that does not meet all of your current needs.

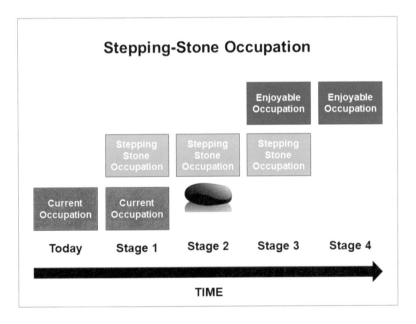

As shown in the diagram, the starting point is today when you are engaging in a current primary occupation that is not meeting your needs for enjoyment and maybe for income or growth. After some research, you decide on a stepping-stone occupation that you can do, preferably part-time. In Stage 1, you add the stepping-stone occupation, which requires maybe 10 hours or so per week of work.

A key characteristic of Stage 1 is that your current occupation serves as a base for the transition while you are simultaneously developing your skills and gaining experience in addition to your current primary occupation. Even though you may not enjoy your current occupation, the reality is usually that you already know how to do your current job and it is generating at least some income. So, in Stage 1 you are not risking everything by quitting your job cold-turkey and praying that it will work starting from the first day. As we will see below, choosing fix-and-flips (for houses in need of repair) can potentially be a viable path for middle-class Americans as a stepping-stone occupation that can be performed about 10 hours or so per week that for many people can match their income of their current occupation within about a year or two if you are very motivated.

When you develop your stepping-stone occupation to the point that it can reliably replace the income of your current primary occupation and you prepare yourself properly, you can proceed to Stage 2 in which you can choose to leave your job or current occupation. In Stage 2, you are relying on the stepping-stone occupation to carry the load of all of your household expenses and finances without the help of your current (first) primary occupation.

During Stage 2, you are preparing and planning the details, logistics, finances, timing, etc. for the transition to Stage 3. In Stage 3, you add your ultimate (or next) enjoyable occupation and get it started while simultaneously engaging in the stepping-stone occupation. The financial base of the stepping-stone occupation should give you the confidence to conservatively plan for and execute the addition of your enjoyable occupation with as little risk as possible. That often means adding the enjoyable occupation slowly and taking small bite-sized pieces of risk in such a way that no single decision or action will be devastating.

Conservative and prudent risk management, including performing deep due diligence on your future enjoyable occupation is key for success in Stage 3. Using a stepping-stone occupation is not free of risk and must be managed very well. If this is scary, it should be. But the alternative is **live with it**. You must make the decision whether to **fix it**, **live with it** or **leave it**. No one else can make that decision for your happiness.

After you have demonstrated a clearly successful track record for the financial viability of your new enjoyable occupation towards the end of Stage 3, you can let go of the stepping-stone occupation, including the financial support that it provided in Stages 2 and 3, then transition into Stage 4. In stage 4, you are relying on your new enjoyable occupation to meet your needs.

To illustrate by example, let's say that you would love to be a professional photographer (or substitute "professional photographer" with your personal choice field of passion) but you're currently stuck in a factory job that you do not enjoy at which you make $60,000 per year. You can learn how to fix-and-flip houses using OPM ("other people's money") by taking a multi-day bootcamp from a house flipping guru with a great track record. You don't need a college degree or even a high school diploma to learn how to do this and many people get started within a few weeks. Let's say that you make a modest $30,000 on your first flip in an affordable real estate market (more than half of US markets in 2022). If it takes 3-6 months to flip such a house (about 1-3 months of actual work, done entirely or mostly by contractors), then if you flip 2 houses per year as a side hustle, you cover your $60,000 per year. Even if you don't enjoy flipping houses, you have created a "stepping-stone occupation" that gives you the opportunity to **<u>fix it</u>** AND **<u>leave it</u>**. Leaving your current non-enjoyable occupation creates the freedom of both time and money so you can enjoy your photography occupation, while also remaining financially viable from flipping houses, in which you leverage other people's money and other people's time.

> **A "stepping-stone occupation" is an occupation that you are likely to enjoy to some extent that will serve as an intermediate step toward eventually engaging in an occupation about which you are likely to be passionate.**

In this example, the stepping-stone occupation is flipping houses for 1-3 years using other people's money (the bank's) and other people's time (contractors to do the work), so you can start to INVEST the rest of your life in the professional photographer occupation about which you are passionate (or any other occupation that you customized to your individual desires).

Be aware that if you don't enjoy flipping houses, you can jettison the stepping-stone occupation (like a NASA booster rocket on the way to the moon) after a few years. In a hypothetical example, you may flip houses for 1-2 years until you are financially confident enough to leave your current occupation, and then continue to flip houses for another 2-5 years while you get your ultimate occupation up and running and stabilized. At that point, you can stop flipping houses if you don't enjoy it or don't need it anymore.

I engaged in active part-time real estate investing over an 11-year period investing in only 1-2 additional houses per year while continuing to enjoy my primary occupation as a chemist. My goal in part-time real estate investing was financial, not happiness. To ensure my happiness, I made sure to avoid driving myself crazy during those 11 years which is why I invested in only 1-2 additional houses per year as a part-time investor. Once I achieved my financial goals, I stopped investing in single-family homes. This is practical for many people in more than half of the United States where real estate prices are relatively affordable, provided that you have a job and reasonable credit, which will enable you to purchase and rehab houses with loans from local portfolio banks, private lenders or hard money lenders. I describe the details of part-time real estate investing in my 27.5-hour "Smarter Investing" home study course (https://vimeo.com/ondemand/smarterinvesting).

Again, I am not saying that real estate investing is the only way to have a stepping-stone occupation, but this happens to be a method that is practical for millions of middle-class Americans with stable jobs that they don't enjoy or that don't meet some other need. Real estate investing doesn't take years to learn and doesn't cost tens of thousands of dollars to get the training. This path may not be viable in other countries for a variety of reasons, but in the United States, part-time real estate investing has been the ticket to financial freedom for MANY people, which can also ultimately lead to psychological freedom as well.[12]

To recap, the flow of the thought process for using a stepping-stone occupation as a path to improve your happiness is based on several assumptions.

First, the assumption here is that you are SPENDING your time at work because you don't enjoy the essence of your work. If you already enjoy the essence of your occupation, this segment is for you only if your motivation is to achieve financial freedom. I want to reemphasize here that my strong bias is that happiness is more important than money.

A second assumption is that you would like to enjoy an occupation so that you can add literally tens of thousands of hours of INVEST time to your life and push your Happiness Score above 68, above 70, above 80 or even above 90.

We will not address here the prudent strategy of diversifying your sources of income as a risk management tool for your financial security, even though that indirectly affects happiness by avoiding financial tension. I have a lecture entitled "How to Achieve Financial Freedom Through Successful Part-Time Investing" in my Smarter Investing training program that describes how to generate full-time income through part-time investing while creating a form of "career insurance." (see www.vimeo.com/ondemand/smarterinvesting).

A third assumption is that you already have in mind a "destination occupation" that you would find enjoyable (very preferably with passion) or that you are open-minded to identifying an occupation that you would enjoy.

---

[12] See Marc Halpern's article on "The Ultimate Investor Endgame" to achieve simultaneous financial and psychological freedom at
https://www.parttimeinvestorsllc.com/single-post/the-ultimate-investor-endgame

The third assumption is necessary because, as described in Chapter 3, we need a destination occupation in order to design an efficient pathway to get from where you are today to where you need to arrive to **BE HAPPIER**.

If you do not already have a destination occupation customized to your personal situation, you can use tools to identify a suitable destination occupation that will improve your happiness with joy and fulfillment at work and maintain financial viability, maybe even financial freedom in the long term.

OPTION 4: START A BUSINESS

Many of the considerations for choosing to start a new business, and choosing which business to start, are the same as described above for changing occupation or using a stepping-stone occupation. On top of all those factors, risk management must be very thoroughly analyzed in writing since the commitment is huge and the ramifications of success and failure are very significant.

Whenever I started a business, including this venture for "Now Be Happier," I always executed the transition while maintaining a stable financial base, such as working at a company (until I became a full-time small business entrepreneur) or using a part-time stepping-stone occupation or part-time stepping-stone small business. I did this to manage risk and avoid financial disaster if the new business failed.

One of the challenges in starting a new business while benefitting from the base of a stable occupation or stable small business is time management. Every person considering taking this leap into starting a business must figure out time management for themselves.

This ties back into Chapter 12 "Happiness in Relationships" since the work/home life balance is crucial. Some ambitious first-time entrepreneurs are so passionately focused on the success of their business that they sacrifice their marriages and families. Before making the decision to start a business, you should strongly consider performing the extremely valuable cost-benefit analysis for every aspect of the venture, including attempting to predict the impact on your relationships and family. It is worth a few hours of analysis? Absolutely yes!

Sometimes, it might be worthwhile to postpone starting a new business until you can achieve a relatively high confidence level that, not only is the business feasible, but that you can also maintain your relationships to be stable at the same time.

For example, writing this book has been in my head for more than 15 years. However, at that time, I was still building my part-time real estate business which was built while maintaining my phase-transfer catalysis consulting business as a stable base. So, I had to postpone the Now Be Happier business platform in order to manage time, minimize risk and simultaneously minimize stress to maintain our stable marriage. That is why I invested in real estate only part-time with only 1-2 additional houses per year. My happy, stable low-stress marriage was MUCH more important than making a boatload of money, which I could have done by scaling the real estate business much faster, like many of my colleagues did. I chose a low-stress life and a stable happy marriage, so I grew my real estate business slowly.

For example, I vowed to NEVER have more than 10 rental units since that was the limit I anticipated I could handle without ruining my happiness. In fact, I peaked at 9 rental units. When I achieved the financial goals from rentals, I then scaled DOWN to 2 rental units in order to increase my psychological freedom (fewer tenants, fewer contractors, no employees, etc.) by redeploying the proceeds from the sales of the rental units into truly 100% passive investments managed by others. Now that I made that transition, I was ready to launch the Now Be Happier platform with the app "**Be Happier**" and the associated website www.NowBeHappier.com, both of which I started about 4-5 years ago. Once my business life was less hectic and while celebrating our 42nd wedding anniversary, I flew to Venice to self-isolate for two weeks and write the first draft of this book.

The lesson from this example is that I always started a new business when I had my other small businesses under control while putting my marriage and family as my #1 top priority. It CAN be done.

To execute this transition and maintain an excellent work-home life balance required hours of strategic analysis. Was it worth it? Absolutely yes! Had I enthusiastically and passionately pushed the Now Be Happier platform to fruition in 2007 or even in 2020, I would have made unacceptable sacrifices to my work/home life balance. I was not willing to pay that high price. So, I analyzed, made decisions and now I am launching the Now Be Happier platform in 2023-4. That worked for me.

What will work for you?

You need to figure that out through a comprehensive analysis of your situation. Your INVESTMENT of the many hours required to perform a thorough **written** analysis, including risk management for both finances and relationships, should yield a tremendous payout for you.

ARE YOU A TEEN OR A PARENT OF TEENS?

Before we conclude this chapter, we recommend a conversation with your teenage children (or from birth if possible) about their initial choice of occupation.

Even though the executive functions in the brain's prefrontal cortex in children are not developed enough to grasp this depth of reason, you can still plant the seed in their heads at an early age that tens of thousands of hours of enjoyable work is so much better than cringeworthy non-enjoyment time at work.

If you are reading this as a young adult who has not chosen your occupation yet, please appreciate your great fortune as you now realize how unbelievably crucial it is to choose an occupation that you enjoy!

Are you old enough to realize that if you enjoy a great home life but don't enjoy your work life, you will be throwing away about 1/3 of your waking hours (40 hours work per week divided by 120 waking hours per week), week after week, month after month, year after year, **decade after decade**. Imagine that! **VERY CRINGEWORTHY!**

Is money an important criterion when choosing an occupation? Yes. But if you haven't yet chosen your occupation, **INVEST 5 minutes to ask a forty- or fifty-year-old who does not derive joy or fulfillment from their job if they wished they made a better choice of occupation**. You probably already know the answer.

HAPPINESS AT WORK - Summary of key points

- When you choose your occupation, **you absolutely must** enjoy your work so that instead of SPENDING time at work, you can INVEST your time at work…FOR MANY TENS OF THOUSANDS OF HOURS OF YOUR LIFE!!!

- Money is an important factor when choosing your occupation, but enjoying your life with fulfillment is more important (assuming you live in a country with enough freedom to pursue happiness).

- For most people, the choice of occupation is the second most important strategic life decision they will make in their entire lifetimes, with relationship choices being the only strategic decision that is usually more important (assuming you live in a country with enough freedom to pursue happiness).

- If you don't currently enjoy your work, you should perform a written analysis to evaluate if you should **fix it, live with it** or **leave it**.

- Regardless of your decision to **fix it, live with it** or **leave it**, perform a comprehensive detailed analysis of the pros, cons, expected outcomes, risk management and practical steps for each potential path.

- Options include:
  o Change boss

- o   Change occupation
- o   Use a "stepping-stone" occupation
- o   Start a business

- Ideally, you should have a stable financial base, a risk management plan and a work/home life balance plan, all in place, before making the transition to change your boss, change your occupation, use a stepping-stone occupation or start a new business.

- Using a part-time stepping-stone occupation, which is a side hustle with manageable risk that is not overly time-consuming, offers more opportunity to successfully manage the risk and the transition than making abrupt occupation changes.

- Changing occupation is a major strategic life decision with huge ramifications for happiness, which can be good (if planned and executed very well) or bad (if poorly planned and/or poorly executed). This is why INVESTING many hours of analysis in writing is crucial.

CHAPTER 14

Happiness and Health

Most people understand that the order of priorities in life is:

1. health
2. happiness
3. prosperity.[13]

Peter Habib is the inspirational chief executive officer of the MPI Family Office and Consortium of Wealth that accumulated $500 million in real estate (https://mpifamilyoffice.com/). He was asked to give advice to a large audience of ultrahigh net worth individuals who were attending the Family Office Super Summit in December 2022. Peter said, "**I have always preached the Healthy Dream Lifestyle that says if you don't have your health, I don't care how much money you guys have, it's no fun**."

While other panel members who were asked for advice talked about how to perform deep due diligence on $100 million deals or "if cash is king then cash flow is queen," Peter Habib chose to first focus on health before money. He was right **not only for ultrawealthy people but for everyone**. Peter then said on stage that our Happiness Score equation "is genius and I want to get the app." Like Peter, many of us agree that health must be the first priority in life, with happiness second and prosperity third.

---

[13] Even though health has a higher priority than happiness in relationships and happiness at work, we address relationships and work earlier in the book than we address health since we usually have near total control over decisions for relationships and work whereas health can be complicated, or even dominated, by external factors beyond our control such as genetics.

You can't enjoy prosperity without health and being healthy is necessary to enjoy happiness without unreasonable barriers.

The table below shows examples of activities in our daily lives for which we can make choices that fall into the categories of INVEST time, SPEND time and WASTE time.

HEALTH	
INVEST	exercise, eat healthy meals, consensual intimacy
SPEND	taking meds,* doctor/dentist visit,* bathroom*
WASTE	smoking, drugs, alcohol in excess, eat unhealthy food, non-consensual intimacy, stress, violence (aggressor or victim)

* unavoidable SPEND time ➜ don't enjoy but would harm if didn't do it

The two most obvious choices we make on a daily basis that affect health for positive INVEST time are food and exercise (assuming that we identify healthy foods we enjoy eating and identify forms of exercise we enjoy)

We probably all know people who during the life-and-death wake-up call of the COVID-19 pandemic decided to take control of their health in 2020-2021. My good friends Dan Zitofsky, Steve Lloyd and Greg Davis set goals for well-being and weight loss during the pandemic and achieved very impressive sustainable results. Not only are the before-and-after pictures of these guys amazing, but their positive attitudes are also contagious and their performance in all aspects of their lives have made them exceptional role models that the rest of us should emulate.

For example, Dan Zitofsky made choices that led to losing 90 pounds in five months and he has maintained that weight loss for more than two years so far! I asked Dan to describe his underlying thought process and I was surprised to learn that his primary goal was to "get healthy long term" and "weight loss was a byproduct." Dan adopted a program developed by a cardiac surgeon to reduce inflammation in the body for true health.[14]

To further understand Dan's choices and mindset, he added "I was a first responder in the 2nd building at 9/11. For the last 20+ years, I've lived with a feeling of guilt that I made it out while others perished. Now as a health coach, I finally understand what my true vision is and why I'm still here. I'm here to bless others with their health to live their best lives." By the way, Dan's primary occupation is in real estate, not health. Dan coaches people for healthy lifestyle as a mission to help others!

An important lesson we can learn from Dan Zitofsky is that everyone is struggling with challenges, sometimes unimaginable challenges, and some people decide to **take control of their lives to enjoy simultaneous health, happiness and prosperity every day for the rest of their lives**. The question is, when facing challenges, are YOU willing to make choices so that YOU can INVEST every minute of the rest of YOUR life instead of SPENDING your life away?

A basic assumption of this book is that YOU control your decisions and actions. Those decisions and actions determine YOUR Happiness Score. Do you want to INVEST your time in life like Peter, Dan, Steve and Greg? If so, what are you going to do about it? How are you going to convert SPEND time and WASTE time into INVEST time?

Another close friend of mine is Renen Avneri. Renen is a top software architect and he wrote the software for the app "**Be Happier**" which you now know is the best way to monitor your Happiness Score and make decisions to **BE HAPPIER**. In high school, Renen weighed 200 kg (440 pounds) and grew up in a single-parent household with low income, though fortunately with very high core values.

Renen decided to "**fix it**" by undergoing surgery and making lifestyle choices that resulted in losing 100 kg (220 pounds)!! I have huge respect and admiration for Renen, his mother Irit and his wife Orit, who have all

---

[14] https://coach.optavia.com/teamdanzito

leveraged their minds and core values to overcome unimaginably difficult challenges.

While Dan, Renen, Steve and Greg made huge changes to their lives with extremely impressive health results, many people are more successful starting with smaller health changes and improving over time. For example, during COVID, I started intermittent fasting and walking 4+ miles per day. I lost 22 pounds (10 kg), which is not as impressive as my friends, but, for more than 3 years, I have maintained the discipline of fasting 16 hours per day and I enjoy my daily walks six days per week on a nature trail near my house while listening to music and podcasts. I'm healthier and happier, although I have a way to go on weight. At the same time, I speculate that my low-stress home life and enjoyable occupation contribute to my good health quite a lot.

Again, the bottom line is that when it comes to health, we can make choices that increase our Happiness Score. While it is unfortunate, and sometimes even tragic, that some health challenges are insurmountable, we must at least try to do whatever we can that is under our control to address the health issue.

Sometimes, we do SPEND time on health activities. Examples include the time SPENT in the dentist's chair to fill a cavity or do a root canal. Few people enjoy these activities but they would result in harm if we didn't do them, which is why going to the dentist is categorized as SPEND time.

As we get older, many of us take medicines to maintain acceptable levels of blood pressure, cholesterol, A1C and other leading indicators used in disease prevention. The few minutes engaged in taking medications every day is SPEND time because it is not exactly enjoyable to swallow pills but many of us believe that harm would result from not taking the medications. If you can avoid taking medications, that's great. However, some people have little choice but to rely on medications such as insulin shots for Type I diabetes or chemotherapy or radiation therapy for cancer.

While we are on the subject of disease or being sick, this is a good time to note that we define the time managing, treating or recovering from illness as SPEND time unless we can simultaneously engage in an enjoyable activity that does not harm ourselves or others.

A perfect example of this, as noted in Chapter 11, is the singer Nightbirde who was able to INVEST time singing and creating beautiful songs for others to enjoy while she was fighting cancer until she succumbed to the disease at the young age of 31.

Certainly, dealing with pain or coping with major medical issues can be so overwhelming that it may seem impossible to INVEST time engaging in enjoyable activities. But with effort and determination, despite illness or pain, the person may still be able to make contributions to their own happiness or the happiness of others. A meaningful, positive and enjoyable contribution, that can even be heroic like in Nightbirde's case, is an example of converting SPEND time into INVEST time, even if only for short periods of time.

Remember, the clock is always ticking, so if we can steal away even a moment of INVEST time in the middle of a long SPEND time event such as an illness, we have achieved an extra moment of happiness. Every extra moment of happiness counts! In the app **"Be Happier,"** every single second of INVEST time **QUITE LITERALLY COUNTS!**

As mentioned earlier, certain activities of personal hygiene, such as using the bathroom, are categorized as SPEND time since the law of conservation of matter dictates that if we didn't eliminate waste from our bodies on a periodic basis, we would explode. Some people have commented that they can convert bathroom time into INVEST time by reading, posting on social media or playing games on their phones during those minutes.[15] One practical characteristic of the way we measure the Happiness Score is that each person can define for

---

[15] https://www.cbsnews.com/detroit/news/study-9-out-of-10-people-use-their-cellular-phone-in-the-bathroom/

themselves how they INVEST, SPEND and WASTE time as long as they are not harming themselves or others.

For me personally, oftentimes my only SPEND time for the day consists of the minutes that I categorize as "Morning Prep". Yes, I tap the yellow SPEND button on the app "**Be Happier**" when I start my personal hygiene "Morning Prep" activities shortly after I wake up and I tap the green INVEST button when I return to engaging in activities that I enjoy such as my occupation or time with my family.

WASTE TIME AND HEALTH

Some choices we make actually result in WASTE time. They include smoking, using illegal drugs (for non-medicinal purposes), drinking alcohol in excess, eating unhealthy food being the aggressor or victim of violence.

All of these activities cause harm to yourself or to others. Any activity that causes harm to you and/or others is WASTE time **by definition**, even if you temporarily enjoy the activity. For example, when drinking alcohol socially at a sporting event or wedding, you must be careful not to cross the line between INVEST time, which might be 1-2 beers, and WASTE time when you get drunk and engage in risky behaviors such as driving drunk, fighting or violating someone's personal intimate space. Some people even use the term getting WASTED to describe getting drunk.

If you are WASTING time, especially with addiction to alcohol, drugs or smoking, you might not need the Happiness Score metric to realize that you need help, although the Happiness Score will force you to stop being in denial. You need to do whatever it takes to safely get help to stop WASTING time engaging in these WASTE time activities. Overcoming dependence and addiction to harmful chemicals (including sugar) is **extremely** difficult and should be treated like a disease since willpower alone often is not enough.

As parents, one of our biggest fears is that our children will engage in harmful behaviors such as taking illegal drugs or be aggressors or victims of violence or violate the personal space of others. We must address these uncomfortable topics with open, age-appropriate communication with our children at all stages of development. Effective dialog is paramount to their safety and well-being. As difficult as these discussions may be, preventing addictions and violence is a whole lot easier than overcoming these experiences after the fact.

During a fraternity pledging event about 20 years ago, a person in our family's sphere of influence died of alcohol poisoning. I cannot imagine the grief of the student's parents. We MUST prepare our children to avoid WASTING time in harmful activities that could literally be a matter of life and death.

One of the most insidious examples of WASTE time related to health is being a victim of physical or verbal abuse. When considering **Fix It**, **Live with It** or **Leave It**, abusive situations may not be easily fixed, however, you must find a SAFE way to disengage from the abuser. This will likely require careful planning and recruiting the help of trusted professionals to escape the abusive situation.

One characteristic of health that we cannot control is the fact that our bodies will ultimately fail one day, hopefully at an old age, no matter how perfectly we manage our health throughout our lifetime. We can exert much control over health by making good choices, but the harsh reality is that we can't avoid eventual total system failure and be immortal. In contrast, when living in a reasonably free society, most of us can exert huge control over our relationships and work and even avoid total failure in these two areas. Unfortunately, we do not have the same control over our bodies. The total failure of our body is an inevitable fact of life (and death).[16]

---

[16] "Remember, being healthy is basically dying as slowly as possible." Ricky Gervais

The temporary nature of the gift of life on earth is all the more reason to make healthy choices and implement healthy life practices, so that we can achieve as much happiness as possible during the time we "rent the earth."

HAPPINESS AND HEALTH - Summary of key points

- Good health is the top priority of life, followed by happiness and then prosperity.

- We can exert a lot of control over our health by making good choices, especially when it comes to food and exercise.

- Some activities of daily life related to health are unavoidable SPEND time activities, such as going to the dentist, using the bathroom and dealing with illness.

- Even when dealing with illness, one can sometimes create opportunities to INVEST time.

- Addictions, violence, abuse and violation of personal space are WASTE time situations in life related to health that can and must be avoided, prevented or overcome. Disengagement from avoidable WASTE time situations can be very difficult and must be done safely, often with the help of trusted licensed professionals.

- Our physical bodies cannot last forever, even if we make perfect choices. However, making good choices related to health will maximize INVEST time, minimize SPEND time and eliminate WASTE time during the finite time you have here on earth.

CHAPTER 15

Customizing Happiness in Other Areas of Your Life

Many other aspects of our lives affect our happiness in addition to happiness in relationships (Chapter 12), happiness at work (Chapter 13) and happiness in health (Chapter 14). Two detailed chapters were dedicated to relationships and work since those two areas represent the majority of our waking hours during every week. Another chapter was dedicated to health since health is the most crucial, necessary but insufficient prerequisite, for happiness in life.

This chapter will provide food for thought for some of the other common aspects of life that are quite important to your overall happiness. This chapter will cover the following topics and each topic will include a quick-reference summary table for INVEST, SPEND and WASTE time.

1. Happiness in Self-Actualization
2. Happiness in Spirituality
3. Happiness in Community
4. Happiness in Activities of Daily Living; Is SPENDING Time Unavoidable?

SELF-ACTUALIZATION

According to the original version of Maslow's Hierarchy of Needs, "self-actualization" is the highest level of human need. Self-actualization includes engaging in activities and achieving accomplishments that make us feel good internally without the need for validation by others.

SELF-ACTUALIZATION	
INVEST	raising children, learning, reading, writing a book, travel, creating art, playing musical instrument, hobbies, mentoring
SPEND	
WASTE	

Some areas of self-actualization involve years of intense activity, such as raising children or developing highly specialized expertise in a chosen field. Other areas for self-actualization can be activities that make you feel good an hour at a time such as reading/learning, cooking, carpentry, gardening, quilting and hundreds of other activities too numerous to mention.

Other areas of self-actualization mix long-term and short-term activities such as playing a musical instrument, mountain climbing, creating works of art, collecting antiques or writing books (like this book).

You should make a list of activities that you enjoy that have nothing to do with impressing other people. They can be hobbies or they can be grand goals such as traveling the world (I have visited 39 countries so far and I enjoy observing other cultures).

Mentoring is an interesting example of INVEST time. Even though other people are involved, being useful and helping others is very rewarding. Mentoring that is motivated by internal satisfaction usually feels much better than mentoring motivated by the desire for recognition or for money.

Write down a list of activities you enjoy for self-actualization and allocate at least some time on a weekly, monthly or annual basis to engage in those activities. Add these activities to your written list in Chapter 7 - "Opportunities to INVEST Time." Every time you engage in an activity of self-actualization that does not cause harm to you or others, you are increasing your INVEST time, which increases your Happiness Score.

SPIRITUALITY

In recent years, a sixth level, spirituality, was added to Maslow's Hierarchy of Needs. Activities of spirituality are usually enjoyed in your brain (or "heart"), though they can be enjoyed in community as well. Two common examples of spiritual INVEST time include prayer and meditation. As long as these activities are done with positive motivation and without causing harm to yourself or others, prayer and meditation can apply to people of all religions or no religion. An example of a secular meditation about **BE HAPPIER** is one that I recorded in Balestrand, Norway in 2018.[17]

SPIRITUALITY	
INVEST	prayer, meditation, charitable work, community worship
SPEND	
WASTE	

Since happiness is about experiencing joy and fulfillment, spiritual activities in which you engage voluntarily that do not cause harm, are INVEST time, which increases your Happiness Score.

COMMUNITY

Many of us supplement our home life and work life activities with community-based activities. Most of these activities are enjoyable most of the time such as cheering for your favorite sports team, which by the way, satisfies Level Three in Maslow's Hierarchy of Needs called "belonging."

Volunteering to help in community activities, such as local food drives, being a leader in Boy Scouts/Girl Scouts, or faith-based initiatives is another way that many of us add meaningful content to our lives. Such

---

[17] Balestrand meditation:
https://vimeo.com/parttimeinvestors/meditationbalestrand#t=14

volunteering is categorized as INVEST time and adds to our self-fulfillment and happiness.

COMMUNITY	
INVEST	volunteering, sports team support, social media*, politics*
SPEND	
WASTE	social media,** politics**

* in moderation and without negativity
** overindulgence harms relationships/productivity; cyberbullying and/or over-negativity harms others

Social media is a double-edged sword right along with politics, depending on whether your motivations and actions are positive or harmful.

Posting cat videos on Facebook and expressing appreciation, empathy or sympathy for friends and family on any appropriate social media platform can be enjoyable and/or encouraging for all involved. Posting "how to" videos for cooking, building things, replacing a car headlight, fixing computer bugs and any other helpful content constitutes INVEST time and adds value for others. Watching and sharing these "how to" videos on social media is INVEST time. These are examples of using social media to INVEST time.

In contrast, cyberbullying and microaggression on social media causes harm and is therefore categorized as WASTE time.

Overindulging in social media can be WASTE time even if you enjoy it. For example, you WASTE time when you are on social media for such an excessive number of hours that it negatively affects your productivity, relationships or sleep. This is the main reason that I deleted Facebook from my laptop and my smartphone. Since Facebook is mostly a social activity for me, I keep Facebook only on my iPad which I use only after work hours. In contrast, I use LinkedIn for work and I am active on LinkedIn on both my smartphone and laptop. Since I enjoy my work, my activity on LinkedIn is always INVEST time.

Engaging in political activity is another area that can be INVEST time or WASTE time.

I must admit that I am cynical about politicians since I perceive (perhaps unjustifiably) that many of them excessively engage in activities to draw attention to themselves, regardless of whether the activities serve the best interests of their constituents. I assume that elected representatives, legislators and others who consider themselves "community leaders" do at least some good for society at least some of the time. When they help society, they are INVESTING time. When they harm society, or even harm selected members of the community, they are WASTING time. When they behave like kindergarten children for perceived personal gain, they are WASTING time.

In principle, when we support harmful politicians, we are WASTING our time as well. The problem is that about 1/3 of adults are positive that the politicians on one side are good, another 1/3 of adults think that the politicians on another side are good and the remaining 1/3 of adults think that politicians on all sides are not good. Unfortunately, there is no objective test to determine which politicians are good or bad (except in extreme cases and even then, there are differences of opinion).

On top of all that, in the age of viral sound bites, attention-getting politicians who behave outrageously often raise more money than "boring" politicians who care more about the welfare of society than their own personal gain.

In other words, politics is one area in which it is extremely difficult to identify objective criteria for causing harm. For that reason, each of us must determine for ourselves if engaging in, or supporting, one form of politics or another represents INVEST time or WASTE time.

OTHER ACTIVITIES OF DAILY LIVING

So far, we have covered happiness in relationships, at work, in health, in self-actualization, in spirituality and in the community. Well, there are many additional mundane activities we perform in our daily lives, sometimes on autopilot. We sometimes don't even notice how much time we INVEST, SPEND or WASTE on these other activities of daily living.

OTHER ACTIVITIES OF DAILY LIVING	
INVEST	gaming*, gardening, watching TV**
SPEND	paying bills, cleaning, fixing things around the house (if you don't enjoy it), mowing the lawn, driving, shopping
WASTE	gaming, ** shopping,*** watching TV,** worrying[18]

* in moderation

** too much time harms relationships/productivity/sleep

*** as escape from problems

Do you enjoy paying bills? I didn't think so. But if you didn't pay bills, you wouldn't have electricity, water, telephone or even a place to live. Paying bills is one of the unavoidable activities in which we SPEND time.

For most of us, cleaning the house is not enjoyable. But if we didn't clean the house or wash the dishes, the resulting unsanitary living conditions might be unhealthy. For most of us, cleaning is considered SPEND time, though there can be joy in observing how beautiful and well-organized the house looks after a thorough cleaning.

I know people who enjoy fixing things around the house. I don't happen to be one of them. For me, fixing things around the house is SPEND time and that is why I outsource most repairs and maintenance to others, so I can **BE HAPPIER**. If you enjoy fixing things around the house or mowing the lawn and taking a moment to admire a job well done, you can choose to categorize these activities as INVEST time.

Determining if engaging in any activity of daily living is INVEST, SPEND or WASTE time, is your own personal choice and is based on

---

[18] Joke: "Worrying works…90% of things I worry about never happen!"

whether you enjoy the activity, don't enjoy the activity that must be done or if doing the activity causes harm.

In November 2022, I presented a TEDx talk at a high school entitled "How to Measure Your Happiness Score and Be Happier."[19] During the Q&A after my lecture, one of the teachers asked if a student playing video games was INVEST time since the students enjoyed gaming though it would sometimes interfere with doing their homework. I responded that gaming represents INVEST time as long as it doesn't cause harm. If excessive gaming by students results in not completing their homework, then the extra incremental time of gaming that interfered with completing home represented WASTE time. In other words, enjoyable gaming that does not cause harm is INVEST time, whereas enjoyable gaming that DOES cause harm is WASTE time.

I use the app "**Be Happier**" religiously every day. I am honest with myself when using the app or else my Happiness Score would be meaningless and not useful. I am 69 years old and my biggest WASTE time activity is related to a bad choice I sometimes make that is somewhat related to my age.

You may know that as one gets older, the biological need to eliminate liquid waste at night increases. When I return to bed from my 1-minute "mass balance" activity at 2:00 am, I sometimes make the poor choice of opening my smartphone and playing one of three games (Rummikub, Wordle or WSOP). This causes me to lose sleep since once I start gaming, I tend to stay awake until I am disciplined enough to stop playing and go back to sleep. When I lose sleep due to making the poor choice to play games at 2:00 am, that is definitely WASTE time.

Since the app "**Be Happier**" forces me to be honest with myself, I am compelled to tap the red WASTE button on the app, BEFORE I open one of the gaming apps on my smartphone in the middle of the night.

---

[19] https://www.youtube.com/watch?v=A9MViB3tS5w

What happens in my mind when I tap the red WASTE button when I start gaming at 2:00 am?

At that moment, I have two choices.

One choice is to say to myself that I am causing harm to myself by not going back to sleep, so I must modify my behavior, NOT open the gaming app and go back to sleep. When I can modify my behavior like that, which is clearly the right choice, I do NOT tap the red WASTE button. I can let the blue SLEEP time segment continue running (assuming that I didn't tap the yellow SPEND button when I got out of bed to go to the bathroom) and I close my eyes and reenter sleep.

But I'm human and I have flaws. Sometimes I make the bad choice and I start gaming in the middle of the night. I may be flawed, but I am still disciplined enough to tap the red WASTE button before opening the gaming app in the middle of the night. In the back of my half-asleep mind, I am aware that I am losing points from my Happiness Score for as long as I am gaming. Yes, I am self-sabotaging my sleep and health by gaming in the middle of the night, but at least I'm honest about it! So, I MUST tap the red button when I self-sabotage. Lying to myself is more unacceptable than the self-sabotage of gaming instead of sleeping.

When I analyze my data on a weekly or monthly basis, the reality of the accumulated WASTE time due to gaming stares me in the face. I then have to make the happiness-changing choice: "Will I continue to WASTE time harming myself by gaming in the middle of the night instead of sleeping or will I choose to modify my behavior and go directly back to sleep after my midnight mass balance activity?"

These are VERY REAL choices and very real questions we each must ask ourselves if we are truly committed to increasing our happiness.

This is exactly why I invented the Happiness Score and worked with my colleague Renen Avneri to launch the app "**Be Happier**." The goal was to help people improve their lives and increase their Happiness Score…including me!

Are any of us perfect? No.

Can we make decisions and take actions to **BE HAPPIER**? Yes. That is the purpose of the app "**Be Happier**."

The clock is ticking whether we are enjoying ourselves, not enjoying ourselves or causing harm. We make choices and they have consequences. You know what choices you make and you know the outcomes of those choices. It's YOUR life. It's YOUR responsibility. You can (should?) enjoy your life as much as possible without causing harm. The app "**Be Happier**" is a tool to help YOU be aware of the choices you make and the outcomes that result from those choices.

Now ask yourself the question, "Is my time watching TV INVEST time or WASTE time?" The answer is likely to be similar to that for gaming. If you're watching TV to wind down a bit after a long day at work and not causing harm (not as an alternative to dinner with family), then that is INVEST time. If you are watching TV instead of investing quality time with family or staying up so late that you're tired at work the next day, that is WASTE time.

What about shopping? I don't enjoy shopping but from time to time I must buy food and fuel the car. For me, shopping is SPEND time. In contrast, some people go shopping to escape certain thoughts or to satisfy some other emotional need. If unnecessary shopping causes harm, such as being overextended financially, then that shopping is WASTE time, while necessary shopping for food is SPEND time if it is not enjoyable.

You really need to be honest with yourself when you categorize your time as INVEST, SPEND, WASTE or SLEEP. If you properly record the time of your activities in one of the four categories, you will not only learn how much you enjoy your life, but you will also identify the areas for improvement of your life which lie in your activities of SPEND time and WASTE time.

The whole purpose of this book is to get you to measure your Happiness Score, identify those activities and time segments in your life that you can change to cause more enjoyment with less harm and **BE HAPPIER!**

SELF-SABOTAGE SUMMARY FOR ACTIVITIES OF DAILY LIVING

Be realistic and acknowledge that you are not perfect, even if you are usually very disciplined. Assuming that you are not perfect, what activities of your daily living are WASTE time? Write down at least one and add it to your written list in Chapter 9 - "Opportunity List to Reduce WASTE Time." If you can identify at least one behavior that causes harm, then you will have **identified an OPPORTUNITY** to increase your Happiness Score!

After you identify an imperfection in your behavior, which is really an opportunity to improve your life, the question that remains is how can you muster up the discipline to stop the self-sabotaging behavior.

I recommend that you watch a 6-minute video on YouTube that you can easily find by searching for the term "Stop It Bob Newhart."[20] Watch this video twice. The first time you watch this video, you will be entertained. Then when you watch the video for the second time, pay attention to the serious message without being distracted by the humor. You will not be sorry when you INVEST your time watching this video twice because you will ENJOY the experience AND you will learn how to eliminate one or more self-sabotaging behaviors from your life, assuming that you are not perfect. Be aware that many people may need the aid of a therapist to stop self-sabotage behaviors. If so, that's OK. It might not be as simple as having Bob Newhart say, "Stop It!"

As a final thought, recognize that no matter how disciplined we are (or want to be), it is impossible to live a life without any SPEND time whatsoever. Even if you are a perfectionist, do not expect to achieve a Happiness Score of 100, unless you intend to be dishonest with yourself.

---

[20] https://youtu.be/Ow0lr63y4Mw

In order to achieve a Happiness Score of 100, you would have to figure out a way to enjoy every single waking minute of your life including time SPENT in Morning Prep, dealing with the inevitable administrative requirements in your life such as paying bills, dealing with the government and coping with medical issues such as going to the dentist.

Customizing HAPPINESS in Other Areas of Life - Summary of key points

- Even though relationships, work and health dominate our waking hours, minutes and seconds, other areas of our lives and activities of daily living must also be counted when measuring our Happiness Score.

- Almost all **self-actualization** activities can be categorized as INVEST time since they are almost always enjoyable to you and do not cause harm.

- Almost all **spirituality** activities can be categorized as INVEST time since they are almost always enjoyable to you and do not cause harm.

- Many, but not all, **community** activities, can be categorized as INVEST time. However, you must be aware that some community activities such as politics and social media can drift into the WASTE time category if they cause harm to you or to others.

- **MANY** other **activities of daily living** can fall into any one of the categories of INVEST, SPEND and WASTE. Examples of unavoidable SPEND activities include paying bills, shopping and cleaning. These are UNAVOIDABLE activities, but can be outsourced if you are simply SPENDING too much time on them provided you can allocate money to pay others to perform these functions for you. Other activities of daily living, such as gaming, can be categorized as INVEST or WASTE, depending on whether you are enjoying the activity without causing harm or enjoying the activity while causing harm.

- Self-sabotage is common, even among people who normally have strong self-discipline. An oversimplified, though sometimes effective method, of overcoming self-sabotaging behaviors is first to be aware of the harmful activity and then simply make the decision to STOP IT. When this oversimplified solution is not feasible, you may need to seek professional help to overcome the self-sabotaging behaviors.

CHAPTER 16

How to Use the App "Be Happier"

You have read a lot about the app "**Be Happier**" throughout this book. Now I will describe how to actually use the app and exactly how it will make the process so easy for you to create your own personal record of the activities and duration that you INVEST, SPEND and WASTE time.

If you haven't already done so, you should download the app "**Be Happier**" from the Apple App Store if you have an iPhone (Android version should be available in the near future).[21] If you don't have an iPhone or if you don't have the app "**Be Happier**", skip to the next chapter for instructions on how to manually track your Happiness Score.

Following are the simple instructions to use the app "**Be Happier**".

- Tap on the green INVEST button when you **START** an activity that you ENJOY that does not cause harm to you or to others.

- Tap on the yellow SPEND button when you **START** an activity that you DON'T ENJOY that would cause harm if you didn't do it.

- Tap on the red WASTE button when you **START** an activity that causes harm to you or to others.

- Tap on the blue SLEEP button when you **GO TO SLEEP**.

---

[21] If you're reading this many years after 2024, iPhone and Android may be history. While there may be other "**Be Happier**" platforms, the principles should remain valid.

The app "**Be Happier**" will automatically keep track of the time between taps and calculate your Happiness Score automatically and continuously. This is an extremely useful and valuable function provided by the app.

In addition, the app will create an "Activities Table" (called "Events Table" in earlier versions) that is shown at the right in the following diagram. In the app "**Be Happier**," you can access the Activities Table by tapping on the "Activities" tab ("Events" tab in earlier versions) at the bottom of the Home screen as represented by the finger pointer on the left side of the diagram.

ACCESSING THE ACTIVITIES TABLE

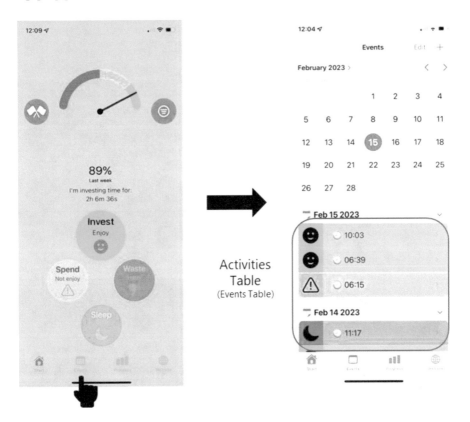

In the diagram above, the Activities Table shows that the user went to sleep at 11:17 pm on February 14. The user woke up at 6:15 am the next morning and started to SPEND time. We will show below that the SPEND time activity that started at 6:15 am was personal hygiene to get ready for the day ("Morning Prep"). The diagram also shows that the user started some enjoyable activity at 6:39 am and another enjoyable activity at 10:03.

In order to understand how you INVEST, SPEND and WASTE your time, it is highly recommended that you NAME each activity in your Activity Table by adding a 1-3 word description.

The next two diagrams show the four easy steps to name an activity. In this example, the user SPENT time on "Morning Prep" from 6:15 am.

Observe the four easy steps (finger pointers #1 to #4) that the user followed to name the SPEND time activity at 6:15 am as "Morning Prep."

4 EASY STEPS TO NAME AN ACTIVITY

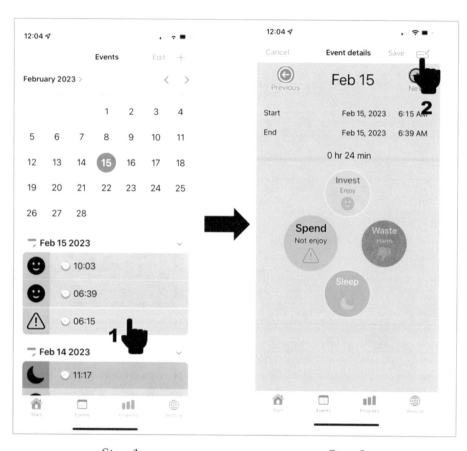

Step 1	Step 2
Tap on the activity	Tap on writing icon

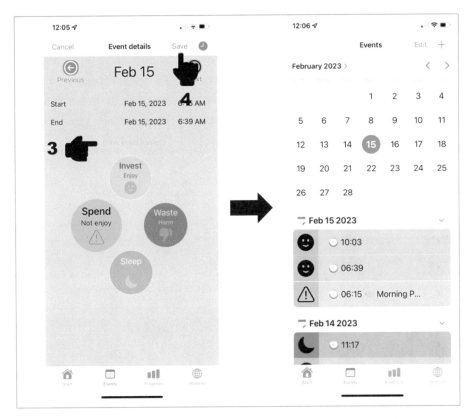

Step 3: Type/Enter name
Step 4: Tap Save

Screenshot after naming 6:15 activity

During the day, if you have named your various activities, such as "Work - Home" and "Project 1", both of which you enjoy without causing harm, your Activity Table screen will change as shown in the three activity tables shown on the next page.

Your activity names will be unique to you, but some common activity names may include: Work, Morning Prep, Exercise, Family Time, Drive to Work, Gaming, Social Media, Cleaning and Pay Bills (or Admin). Be consistent with naming activities since that will be important when we discuss the very powerful Opportunity Table later in Chapter 18. To further personalize the app, you can also use keyboards for different alphabets and languages.

In addition to the flexibility of naming your own activities, the app "**Be Happier**" allows YOU to determine whether the activity is INVEST time, SPEND time, or WASTE time, because different people will tap different buttons for the same activity. I tap the green INVEST button for almost all of my work because I enjoy that work. You might tap the yellow SPEND button when you start working if you don't enjoy your work.

TRACKING YOUR DAY BY NAMING YOUR ACTIVITIES ON THE ACTIVITY TABLE

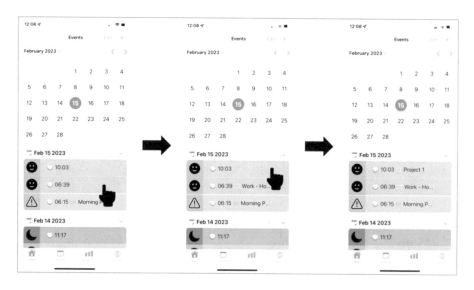

Recommendation: While it is not necessary, it is worthwhile to record new activities and name them separately even when you transition from one INVEST activity to another INVEST activity even though you enjoy both activities! This will help you identify which activities you may want to maximize going forward. It's also uplifting to realize that you might be enjoying your life more than you previously perceived.

Let's discuss an example of how to use the app "**Be Happier**" more effectively by giving appropriate names to activities (events) for one of the most important categories of life, which is work.

TWO JOBS OR A "SIDE HUSTLE"

This example refers to the millions of people who have two jobs or a primary occupation plus a side hustle and/or a "stepping-stone occupation" described in Chapter 13. **The guideline is to name the time you INVEST or SPEND at each job or side hustle SEPARATELY, instead of just using one activity name like "Work."**

I am one of those many people with multiple occupations. When I start doing work in my primary occupation of phase-transfer catalysis (PTC), which I enjoy immensely, I tap the green INVEST button. I then NAME the activity (event) in the Activity Table by tapping on the Activities tab in the tab bar and editing the name to "PTC," as described earlier.

In contrast, when I am doing part-time work to manage my single-family home rentals (my side hustle), which I **sometimes do NOT enjoy** but that produces semi-passive income and grows my net worth, I tap the yellow SPEND button as soon as I start turning my attention only to those specific activities that I do not enjoy. I name the activity (event) as "Rentals." Fortunately, I no longer SPEND more than about an hour or two per month (on average) on activities for my rentals that I don't enjoy. This is one reason why my Happiness Score THESE DAYS is usually in the 90's. It wasn't always that way and in Chapter 18, I will show how I used my detailed data to support a major change in my life which was to sell my rentals.

In other words, when we are more specific in naming our various activities, we get a better picture of how we are INVESTING, SPENDING and WASTING our time in reality. You may be surprised to find out how much time you really are INVESTING or SPENDING at your primary occupation, your side hustle, with friends, on social media, etc.

Once you are aware of how you are INVESTING, SPENDING and WASTING your time, you are MUCH more likely to make changes to improve your life.

USING THE SLEEP BUTTON

As we discussed in Chapter 10 - SLEEP, we tap on the blue SLEEP button when we go to sleep. Perhaps in the future, the app or some other device (like an Apple watch if we wear it to sleep) may be able to determine by itself when we start to sleep, but until then, we have no choice but to tap on the blue SLEEP button in the app "**Be Happier**" while we are still awake. We obviously cannot tap on a button when we are asleep and unconscious.

If you wake up in the morning and realize that you forgot to tap the SLEEP button when you went to sleep the night before, you can use the Activities Table to add an activity (event) and edit it with the start time and end time. In fact, that happens to me at least once per week and I estimate the time that I went to sleep the night before.

You may be worried that the exact measurement of the hours and minutes of sleep is not accurate and might mess up your Happiness Score. In fact, some people fall asleep quickly after "going to sleep" while others take a while to fall asleep and some people take a very long time to fall asleep. The app "**Be Happier**" is not intended to serve as a sleep monitor and it turns out that the arithmetic of the Happiness Score does not require exact measurement of hours and minutes of sleep in order to be practical.

Why?

The answer requires examining the arithmetic of the Happiness Score described in Chapter 4 and understanding the choice of "two significant digits" discussed in Chapter 7. If you have patience to understand the arithmetic of the Happiness Score Equation in Chapter 4, please read the rest of this paragraph. If not, skip to the next paragraph. Note that the impact of SLEEP appears only in the denominator of the Happiness Score. Accordingly, an incorrect recording of sleep time by, say 15 minutes, will not change the Happiness Score enough to change the second significant digit of the score. An incorrect measurement of 15 minutes per night is 105 minutes per week or 1.75 hours per week. Since there are 168 hours in a week, an incorrect value of 15 minutes per night moves the needle by only 1%.

In layman's terms, if we record a time that we go to sleep that is off by up to 15 minutes every night, it doesn't affect the Happiness Score by very much and it is not enough to make a difference on the conclusions you reach for making changes in your life.

In summary, SLEEP is a very important aspect of life. SLEEP is also a factor used to calculate the Happiness Score. For those reasons, it is important to tap the SLEEP button when we go to sleep and tap an appropriate button when we wake up for INVEST, SPEND or WASTE. However, it turns out that the perfectly accurate measurement of SLEEP is not crucial to leverage the power of the app "**Be Happier**" even though it is important to be much more accurate when recording your activities of INVEST, SPEND and WASTE. Do not rely on the app "**Be Happier**" to track your sleep accurately. There are other apps for that.

YOUR NEXT POWERFUL STEP! THE OPPORTUNITY TABLE!

You have learned many things by reading this book so far.

- You learned the importance and definitions of INVEST time, SPEND time and WASTE time.

- You learned to ask the SPEND-to-INVEST Question that enables you to make changes in your life, both big and small, to increase your Happiness Score and **BE HAPPIER**.

- You read examples of how to convert SPEND time to INVEST time and how to minimize WASTE time.

- You just learned how to use the free app "**Be Happier**" in order to measure your Happiness Score which enables you to monitor your progress as you convert SPEND and WASTE time into INVEST time.

The next powerful concept you will learn is called "The Opportunity Table." The Opportunity Table is a very practical tool that will turbocharge the impact of measuring your Happiness Score.

How?

Your Opportunity Table identifies and ranks exactly which activities you need to improve and gives the details of your progress.

Sounds great?

The Opportunity Table is so powerful that Chapter 18 is dedicated to showing you how the Opportunity Table works.

Chapter 18 will also show examples of using the Opportunity Table to make major changes that result in a **huge impact on quality of life for years and decades**. If you have the app "**Be Happier**," skip to Chapter 18 now.

CHAPTER 17

How to Track Your Happiness Score Manually (Without the App)

You do <u>NOT</u> need the app "**Be Happier**" on your smartphone to enjoy all of the benefits of measuring your Happiness Score!

You <u>CAN</u> **manually** track your activities and time that are the basis for your Happiness Score. It takes some effort and the effort is worth it since you agreed in Chapter 1 that your goal is to **BE HAPPIER**.

The instructions are simple.

Create the "Activity Table" using the template shown below. You can use spreadsheet software or you can do this with pen and paper, for example in a journal. Some of you may already be journaling, so creating your written Activity Table will fit naturally into your daily routine.

ACTIVITY TABLE

Date			
Start Time	**Activity Name**	**I, S, W, Sleep**	**Duration**

On most days, you will need a minimum of two rows in your Activity Table, one to record when you go to SLEEP and one to record your activity when you wake up.

You can decide how many rows you need in your Activity Table on a given day based on how detailed you want to record your activities. I have been using the app "**Be Happier**" and its test versions for a few years and I rarely have more than eight activities in my Activity Table on any given day.

The most important action you must take to measure your Happiness Score as you proceed through your day is to simply record the start time and activity name in the Activity Table when you **START** the activity. After doing this a few times, you will see that it is not hard at all and does not consume much time (approximately 10 seconds each time).

> **As you proceed through your day, simply record the start time and activity name in your Activity Table when you <u>START</u> the activity. After doing this a few times, you will see that it is not hard at all and takes only about 10 seconds each time.**

You should also invest another second or two to record in the third column whether the activity is INVEST (I), SPEND (S), WASTE (W) or SLEEP.

When you record the start time and activity name of the NEXT activity, that will provide you with the information you need to calculate and enter the duration of the previous activity in the fourth column of the Activity Table.

If you are recording these items in writing with pen and paper (or in a journal), you can tally the durations of each activity at the end of the day when you might have more time than on the fly during your busy day.

If you are using a spreadsheet to record the start time, activity name and I/S/W/Sleep, you can set up your spreadsheet to automatically calculate the duration and automatically enter that into the fourth column.

If you are recording your entries in the Activity Table with pen and paper, you will likely find it easiest to tally your total time of INVEST, SPEND, WASTE and SLEEP on a weekly basis. Then tally your results at the end of the weekend using the following template that you can complete every Sunday night. This is practical since weekdays are different than weekends due to your different activities at work and at home.

7-Day Totals	hrs:min	
INVEST		
SPEND		
WASTE		
Total wake time		= I + S + W
INVEST minus WASTE (I-W)		
HAPPINESS SCORE		= (I-W) / Total wake time
SLEEP		

You may also want to create a tally sheet for every 4-week period in order to monitor the progress of your Happiness Score.

If you are recording your entries in spreadsheet software, you can easily set up your spreadsheet to **automatically** tally your total time of INVEST, SPEND, WASTE and SLEEP on an **ongoing basis**, such as a running 3-day, running 7-day, running 30-day period or all of the above.

Obviously, if you have an iPhone or if the app "**Be Happier**" is available on Android or other platform when you read this book, it is much easier to download the free app "**Be Happier**" and save yourself the time and effort to record all of these entries and perform the very simple arithmetic. This was described in the previous chapter.

Since you have read this far in this book, you obviously see the value in measuring your Happiness Score and leveraging your awareness of your Happiness Score to modify your behavior and take action to improve your life.

At this point, you need to decide if it is worthwhile to invest less than a minute a few times each day to record your entries in the Activity Table so you can monitor your progress as you take action to **BE HAPPIER**.

> **At this point, you need to decide if it is worthwhile to invest less than a minute a few times each day to record your entries in an Activity Table so you can monitor your progress as you take action to BE HAPPIER.**

If you decided that it IS worthwhile to record your entries, you will be amazed at what you can do with your data to turbo-charge the impact of measuring your Happiness Score.

How?

Read the next chapter on The Opportunity Table! It's powerful!

CHAPTER 18

How to Use the Opportunity Table to BE HAPPIER

This chapter will show you an extremely practical tool that will greatly help you to **BE HAPPIER**. This tool is "The Opportunity Table."

You know that in order to **BE HAPPIER**, you must transfer seconds of your life from the SPEND and WASTE categories to the INVEST category.

Imagine how much **YOU** could increase **YOUR** Happiness Score and improve **YOUR** life if you had a personal, customized and ranked list that told you how much time you SPEND and WASTE on specific activities!

Your Opportunity Table is a practical roadmap that **EXPLICITLY IDENTIFIES AND RANKS** which activities in your life you don't enjoy (SPEND) or cause harm (WASTE).

The ranking of these activities is very important because once you are aware of exactly how much time you are SPENDING or WASTING on each specific activity, Your Opportunity Table **prioritizes** for you which activities you need to address so you can make changes to improve your life.

The Opportunity Table is a ranked list of **YOUR** top activities of SPEND time and WASTE time in the past 30 days (or 7 days when you first start) expressed in hours (and minutes). The activity with the most hours is shown on top, regardless of whether it is SPEND time or WASTE time.

The activities are listed in order of decreasing SPEND time or WASTE time.

The blank Opportunity Table looks like this:

Opportunity Rank	SPEND or WASTE	Activity Name	Time During Past 30 Days
1			
2			
3			
4			
5			
6			
7			
8			
9			
10			
11			
12			

We will show you later in this chapter how to manually construct your personal Opportunity Table whether you have the app **"Be Happier"** or not.

An example of an Opportunity Table is shown below for a **hypothetical person** who manages his/her life with several glaring opportunities: [1] SPENDS time at work he/she doesn't enjoy, [2] WASTES too much time on social media instead of productive activities or SLEEP and [3] WASTES too much time gaming instead of productive activities or SLEEP. Social media and gaming are OK to a point, but the time WASTED on social media and gaming is time well beyond that needed for relaxation.

Let's examine the Opportunity Table of this hypothetical person in order to formulate a plan to improve their life.

First, this person appears to go to work to make money with little joy, fulfillment or sense of accomplishment. Based on Chapter 13, this Opportunity Table clearly suggests that changing jobs or changing occupations (possibly through a stepping-stone occupation) should be a top priority to improve happiness during their temporary time on earth.

OPPORTUNITY TABLE

Sample

Opportunity Rank	SPEND or WASTE	Activity Name	Time During Past 30 Days
1	SPEND	Work	160 h 21 min
2	WASTE	Social Media Excess	62 h 35 min
3	WASTE	Gaming Excess	45 h 13 min
4	SPEND	Drive to Work	23 h 06 min
5	SPEND	Morning Prep	17 h 25 min
6	SPEND	Cleaning	12 h 57 min
7	SPEND	Shopping	9 h 49 min
8	SPEND	Mow Lawn	8 h 32 min
9	SPEND	Pay Bills	5 h 11 min
10	SPEND	Headache	4 h 43 min
11	WASTE	Arguing-Yelling	3 h 19 min
12	WASTE	Alcohol Excess	2 h 16 min

Millions of people in this situation simply resign themselves to the reality that they don't enjoy their job and they decide to **live with it**.

Here is where measuring your Happiness Score (with or without the app **"Be Happier"**) can be used to change this person's life. When no action is taken to change their work situation, their Happiness Score will remain unchanged and stagnate month after month, year after year. This person will be reminded of this every time they look at their Happiness Score (immediately as soon as they open the app **"Be Happier"**) until they get sick and tired of seeing their low Happiness Score to the point that they will be motivated to look for a better employer or seriously consider starting a new business or make a transition with a stepping-stone occupation.

If this person finds a better employer that provides a less stressful work environment that additionally shows appreciation for a job well done and a pay raise due to a better fit of personal talents to the requirements of the new job, that person's Happiness Score might jump 30 points within weeks of taking action!

When this person moves to a more fulfilling job, the item "Work" may even disappear from the Opportunity Table!

This person may also be surprised by the second-ranked item in the Opportunity Table. Now that the person has a happier reality, they might not feel the need to escape so many excess hours into the world of social media (or excess alcohol). That might result in another nice bump up in the Happiness Score.

In other words, when we change our lives to **BE HAPPIER** while monitoring our Happiness Score and examining our Opportunity Table, we will see <u>MEASURABLE RESULTS</u> in both the Happiness Score and in the Opportunity Table! We should celebrate the victories of changes of a few points in the Happiness Score and/or reducing the hours of items in the Opportunity Table.

The Opportunity Table is a tool that turbo-charges the impact of measuring your Happiness Score.

What are the different roles of your Happiness Score and your Opportunity Table? Your Happiness Score measures your overall level of happiness. It takes into account ALL of your various activities and whether you enjoy them (INVEST), don't enjoy them (SPEND) or cause harm (WASTE).

In contrast, your Opportunity Table explicitly identifies and ranks which activities in your life you don't enjoy (SPEND) or cause harm (WASTE). <u>The Opportunity Table is where the rubber meets the road</u>.

Both your Happiness Score and your Opportunity Table objectively show your measurable progress along your journey to **BE HAPPIER**. Your Happiness Score shows your overall progress at a glance. Your Opportunity Table gives you the details of your progress, though it requires a bit of extra effort to create and modify from time to time.

It's now time to learn how to create your own personal Opportunity Table.

HOW TO CREATE YOUR OPPORTUNITY TABLE

There are two ways to create your Opportunity Table.

1. One method is passive = you invest very little effort using the app "**Be Happier**" (Note: this is a premium feature).

2. The other method is active = you manually track and compile your time and activities. Don't worry, it's not hard and it's free.

Important Note #1: Whether you have the app "**Be Happier**" or not, you should learn how to create the Opportunity Table manually because the passive method is not available to everyone.

Important Note #2: Be aware that the passive and automatic creation of the Opportunity Table is a premium feature of the app "**Be Happier**" that requires an upgrade at a nominal cost for convenience after an initial trial period.

In the next few paragraphs, you will see that the extra effort is not very much to create your Opportunity Table from your data that are used to measure your Happiness Score. You really can do it yourself easily WITHOUT the premium feature of the app "**Be Happier.**"

The nominal cost for the convenience of passive, automatic and continuous updating of your Opportunity Table helps fund the ongoing support for the basic free app "**Be Happier.**" We want to maintain the basic app "**Be Happier**" as a **FREE service** to enable people around the world to **BE HAPPIER**, especially people with limited resources.

We believe that it is a basic human right to **BE HAPPIER**. We support that basic human right by providing the app "**Be Happier**" free of charge. We feel that it is fair to help fund the support of the free app for the masses with a small convenience fee for the passive generation of the Opportunity Table.

> **Your Opportunity Table turbo-charges the impact of measuring your Happiness Score.**
>
> **Your Happiness Score measures your overall happiness and progress.**
>
> **Your Opportunity Table identifies and ranks exactly which activities you need to improve and gives the details of your progress.**

We will now show you how to manually construct your Opportunity Table if you have the free app "**Be Happier**" or if you are recording your activities without the app in a spreadsheet or in a journal.

STEPS TO CREATE YOUR OPPORTUNITY TABLE

Step 1: Scroll through the past 30 days of your Activity Table. It doesn't matter if you created your Activity Table manually, in spreadsheet software or if the free app "**Be Happier**" created it for you.

Step 2: Write down the names of the activities that were SPEND time or WASTE time during the past 30 days.

Skip over ALL activities of INVEST time since the opportunities are in the SPEND and WASTE time activities.

Step 3: Add up all the hours and minutes for each activity of SPEND time and WASTE time during those 30 days.

Step 4: Record the top entries in the Opportunity Table ranked from highest total time to lowest total time.

Opportunity Rank	SPEND or WASTE	Activity Name	Time During Past 30 Days
1			
2			
3			
4			
5			
6			
7			
8			
9			
10			
11			
12			

That's it! You now have your personal, customized, ranked Opportunity Table!

The Opportunity Table very clearly informs you which activities you don't enjoy or cause harm that you can address to improve your life!

Just as we explained at the beginning of Chapter 3 when using a GPS app, "If you don't know where you are now OR if you don't know where you're going, there is no way that the GPS app can tell you the most efficient path to take."

The Opportunity Table tells you where you are at that moment and clearly lays out in front of you, which activities you need to improve with the specific data about **YOUR** life in the real world so you can make decisions, change your behaviors and **BE HAPPIER**!

> **The Opportunity Ranking Table will very clearly inform you which activities you don't enjoy or cause harm that you can address to improve your life!**

EXAMPLE — MAJOR WORK-LIFE CHANGE

I will describe how I made a major strategic change to my work life when faced with the stark reality forced in my face by the Opportunity Table when I was first developing the concept. Note how a key factor in this success was to assign different names to different types of work.

Many of you will recognize this situation that you face at work, especially if you have a side hustle.

In Chapter 16, I described how I immensely enjoy my work in the field of PTC, but I didn't always enjoy my side hustle which was managing several single-family rental homes that generated semi-passive income. I made an extremely important strategic life decision when I was faced with the reality of how many hours per month I was SPENDING managing certain activities for my rentals (even though I did enjoy some of the activities).

When we started developing the first working versions of the app "**Be Happier**" in 2019, I found myself tapping the yellow SPEND button almost every time I dealt with tenants in 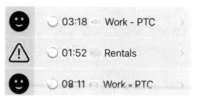 the rentals. A relevant portion of my Activities Table (then called "Events Table") looked like the one shown at the right on a certain workday. As you can see, the time I was SPENDING that day dealing with tenants ("Rentals") interrupted my time that I was INVESTING in the enjoyable intellectually stimulating work of my primary occupation ("PTC").

I wanted the income and growth in value of those rentals to contribute to the financial stability of my family. **But my first attempts to manually construct an Opportunity Table as described above, forced me to ask myself "How could I reduce the 5 or so hours per week I was SPENDING** on the rentals while still maintaining the income and growth they provided?"

After studying my options, I started selling my rentals in 2019, since I did not enjoy all aspects of managing them. Then I redeployed the proceeds of the sales into private placement investments that are 100% totally passive (managed by others, after due diligence) and have similar income and growth.

The net result of this very important strategic life decision was that **I greatly reduced my SPEND time** while today I maintain a higher level of income and growth. In other words, I leveraged my knowledge of how much time I SPENT managing rentals to make a change to "have my cake and eat it too." I now SPEND only about an hour or two per month on average managing aspects of my two remaining rentals that I do not enjoy. I credit the app "**Be Happier**" and the Opportunity Table for clearly showing me that I needed to make a major change in my work life.

Let's calculate. I reduced the time I SPEND on rentals from about 20 hours per month to about 2 hours per month. That is a 90% reduction in my SPEND time per month for this one activity!

Of course, one must consider various options to answer the SPEND-to-INVEST Question as described in Chapter 8. Another option was to hire a property manager to manage the rentals instead of self-managing them, which was a less desirable option since the property management fee of 8% or so represented about 30% of the profit and I would still have the hassle of owning rental real estate and managing the property manager. After considering my options, I decided to sell the rentals and **BE HAPPIER**.

At the time of writing this book, I have only two single-family home rentals left (one with outstanding 17-year tenants) and I expect to sell one from my LLC soon and **BE HAPPIER**!

The transition from part-time single-family home investing that is semi-passive to much more passive private placement investing has been so successful that I now teach successful mom-and-pop landlords how to achieve simultaneous "financial AND psychological freedom" in a program I call "The Ultimate Passive Investor Endgame."[22]

The point is that **analyzing your SPEND time and WASTE time can have great impact on your happiness** when you simply do the following:

1. Measure your Happiness Score.

---

[22] https://www.parttimeinvestorsllc.com/single-post/the-ultimate-investor-endgame

2. Name your activities.

3. Analyze **YOUR** data for INVEST, SPEND and WASTE time.

4. Compose your Opportunity Table.

5. Take appropriate action based on the reality that stares you in the face when you are aware of **YOUR** SPEND and WASTE data in **YOUR** real world.

I found that I greatly enjoy my new side hustle of evaluating private placements from the comfort of my armchair. Reading these investment offerings in many different fields is very interesting and intellectually stimulating, so I tap the green INVEST button and name the activity "PPM" (for private placement memorandum) whenever I engage in this activity.

This is a real-life example of how I graduated from one life stage to another and continuously improved my happiness without sacrificing my financial status. It was 100% based on converting my SPEND time managing rentals that I did not always enjoy, to INVEST time evaluating private placement investments that I do enjoy, while at the same time improving my financial status!

I know that many of you have not yet achieved financial freedom and you might be saying to yourself that my example described above is out of touch with the reality of your situation. Know that my growing family was under the federal poverty level on my 30th birthday and I had to advance through the same stages of life that most of you are experiencing. **The trick was graduating from one life stage to another while simultaneously enjoying my family, my occupation and my financial status**. One credential for writing this book, other than inventing the Happiness Score model, is that I achieved exactly that simultaneous growth in happiness and prosperity along the journey and I did it by making excellent strategic decisions, always keeping happiness in the forefront of those decisions.

I started investing in real estate part-time at age 50 to supplement my retirement planning. Many of you will perceive that is a late age to start and you're right. But it **CAN** be done. Not only can it be done financially, but it can be done while maintaining a high level of happiness.

How? I made the strategic decision **FOR HAPPINESS SAKE** to avoid driving myself crazy, which meant investing part-time on purpose, buying only 1-2 houses per year (usually using other people's money, OPM). I could have made MUCH more money, MUCH faster by immersing myself in real estate investing, like many of my colleagues did. Instead, I chose to INVEST more time with family and INVEST time in my enjoyable primary occupation, rather than jeopardize my stable family, had I chosen to make more money faster. I "had my cake and ate it too," along the journey to simultaneous happiness and prosperity. I am living proof that it **CAN** be done!

The point in telling you my story was to emphasize that we can achieve excellent work-life balance but we must be aware of exactly how we are INVESTING or SPENDING our time at work, at home and in all other activities. The Opportunity Table shows us exactly where our greatest potential opportunities exist for major life change, especially those that can convert SPEND time into INVEST time that can actually be practical.

Let's refocus on you right now. Are you enjoying how you make money? Are you INVESTING time at work or SPENDING time at work? How many hours are you SPENDING or INVESTING in your side hustle?

Using the app "**Be Happier**" will bring your work-life happiness into focus. That's about 1/3 of your waking hours! A few taps per day on the app "**Be Happier**" will empower you to come to grips with optimizing thousands of hours of your future life until you retire.

Measuring your Happiness Score on a continuous basis, monitoring your Opportunity Table and taking action in well-defined activities of life can result in a major improvement in your life! Are you willing to engage your brain to do this? Is measuring your Happiness Score and creating your Opportunity Table such a hassle that it is not worth the benefit of improving the next years and decades of your life?

Using the app "Be Happier" will bring your work-life happiness into focus. That's about 1/3 of your waking hours!

Do you want to optimize thousands of hours of your future life until you retire?

We are making it easy with the free app "**Be Happier**" and it is not that much work to construct the Opportunity Table manually without the app. Do you have an excuse for doing nothing and **living with it**?

It's YOUR life! It's YOUR choice! Monitoring your Happiness Score and Opportunity Table is not hard!

SET YOUR GOALS AND MONITOR YOUR PROGRESS

If your Happiness Score is less than 90, and especially if it is less than 75, you now have the opportunity to change many tens of thousands of hours of the rest of your life!

If your Happiness Score is currently less than 50, perhaps you should consider setting a goal that your Happiness Score will increase to 70 within 3 years and to 90 within 5 years.

Remember that in Chapter 3 we pointed out the obvious that a GPS app cannot take you to a destination if the destination is not known!

Do you really want to **BE HAPPIER**?

If so, what does that mean?

> **Measuring your Happiness Score on a continuous basis, monitoring your Opportunity Table and taking action in well-defined activities of life can result in a major improvement in your life!**

The Happiness Score gives you a golden opportunity to set a measurable goal for increasing your happiness. Imagine celebrating every time your Happiness Score increases by 5 points! That's a big deal.

Maybe you can increase your Happiness Score by safely making changes that result in better relationships, including eliminating toxic relationships from your life. The clock is ticking.

Maybe you can increase your Happiness Score by safely making changes to your employment that result in a happier work environment or even a much more enjoyable occupation for the rest of your life! The clock is ticking and it doesn't tick backwards. Do you constantly complain about your boss or your job? If so, that means that your Happiness Score is not as good as it should be. Are you going to **fix it**, **live with it** or **leave it**? Imagine how you will feel if and when you actually **fix it**!

Your Happiness Score will alert you to your overall level of happiness. **Your Opportunity Table will pinpoint WHERE to look to increase your Happiness Score and BE HAPPIER**.

Unless you live in a totalitarian society with no freedom or you are in a dangerously abusive relationship, you have the ability to take more control of your life and **BE HAPPIER!**

If you don't take advantage of measuring your Happiness Score, set a Happiness Score goal and make changes to **BE HAPPIER**, you better have a good REASON, because an excuse will not cut it!

What a shame it would be if you have the ability to **BE HAPPIER** and you squandered the opportunity due to laziness or inertia. Maybe reading this book is your wake-up call.

The clock is ticking whether you're happy or not.

You might as well **BE HAPPIER** from now and for every moment of the rest of your life, which by the way is irreversible.

It's your choice to **BE HAPPIER**.

This is your opportunity.

NOW BE HAPPIER!

The Opportunity Table - Summary of Key Points

- Your Opportunity Table is a practical roadmap that EXPLICITLY IDENTIFIES AND RANKS which activities in your life you don't enjoy (SPEND) or cause harm (WASTE).

- Armed with the awareness of the activities in which you SPEND the **most** time and WASTE the **most** time, you can prioritize those activities you need to improve as opposed to being overwhelmed by the multitude of items that need improvement in your life.

- As you reduce the time you SPEND and WASTE on even one item in your Opportunity Table, you will see progress in a higher Happiness Score and reduced time in the Opportunity Table.

- Celebrate these real, measurable and tangible victories.

- The minimal effort to diligently use the app "**Be Happier**" and monitor your Opportunity Table is strongly justified as you experience the clearly observable improvement in your happiness.

Shown below is a screenshot of the home screen of the premium version of the app "**Be Happier**" as of the date of this publication. The home screen may change as the app is updated periodically.

Note the presence of the "Opportunity Table" icon in the tab section at the bottom of the screen.

Remember that you can manually create and monitor your personal Opportunity Table as described earlier in this chapter. The automatic and continuous generation of your Opportunity Table is only a convenience which is why it is a premium feature at a nominal fee for the app "**Be Happier**." As explained earlier, the nominal fee for the Opportunity Table optional premium feature helps fund ongoing support for the app "**Be Happier**" so that people with little resources can continue to use the very practical and functional free app to improve their lives and **BE HAPPIER!**

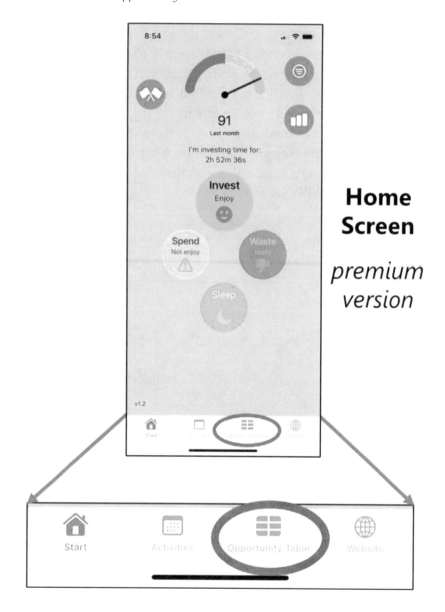

Home Screen

premium version

Example of Actual Opportunity Table with Premium App Shown for "Past Month"

Opportunity Table			
👎	#1	Internet	15:56:54
⚠	#2	Recovery	11:09:58
⚠	#3	Pay bills	3:35:28
⚠	#4	Rentals	2:02:00
⚠	#5	Morning Prep	1:48:06
⚠	#6	Car Maintenance	41:28
⚠	#7	Accounting	20:04

Start   Activities   Opportunity Table   Website

Note that this user enjoys their primary occupation, so this Opportunity Table has no work-related SPEND time, other than "Rentals" that involves dealing with tenants in their side-hustle.

In this case "Internet" was defined by the user as WASTE time gaming, browsing the web, watching YouTube or reading Email between 11:00 pm and 6:00 am when the user should have been sleeping. "Recovery" was the term used by the user when having a headache or being sick.

Clearly, the biggest OPPORTUNITY in this Opportunity Table is to assert more self-discipline to stop opening the smartphone or tablet instead of sleeping in the middle of the night. The user WASTED nearly 16 hours in the past month on "Internet." That represents a lot of self-harm that should be corrected! The user can monitor progress (or regression!) in both the Happiness Score and in the Opportunity Table. In case you haven't already guessed it, this user is me.

CHAPTER 19

Summary and Action Plan

You have probably heard the saying "You only live once" (YOLO). I recently heard a better version which is, "You only DIE ONCE but <u>YOU LIVE EVERY DAY</u>."

The question is, "How do you want to live every day?" This question is about every minute of the rest of YOUR life. That's a very serious question!

This summary and your personal action plan depend on your Happiness Score and your personal components of INVEST time, SPEND time and WASTE time that contribute to your Happiness Score.

HAPPINESS SCORE MORE THAN 90

A few of you have a Happiness Score above 90. Congratulations! You likely have a very good home life, good relationships, a satisfying occupation and you likely have a good handle on managing irritations in life. You likely don't need any major course corrections. In fact, you may have difficulty finding opportunities to squeeze out some very minor course corrections to convert the small amounts that you SPEND time or WASTE time into INVEST time or SLEEP. Your Opportunity Table will point out the few areas in which you may be able to make those minor course corrections. Your Happiness Score is consistently in the green zone except during occasional transient emergencies.

I happen to be in the green zone almost all of the time these days (the figure shown a couple of pages ago is my actual screenshot of the app on this day of writing and shows a Happiness Score of 94, NOT 100!).

However, in my early life, I was nowhere near the green zone, like most of you. Even today, I certainly am not perfect and my Opportunity Table shows some self-sabotage by excessive internet, social media and gaming as WASTE time instead of SLEEP in the middle of the night. This is where I must improve to **BE HAPPIER** and I am working on better discipline in this specific area. What does YOUR Opportunity Table show?

HAPPINESS SCORE 75-90

Many of you, though not a majority, have a Happiness Score of 75-90. You are doing relatively well but could still improve your life by using your Opportunity Table to identify a few course corrections that are likely minor, mostly converting a few irritating SPEND time activities and maybe a few self-sabotage WASTE time activities into INVEST time or SLEEP. You likely don't hate your occupation or else your Happiness Score couldn't be in the 70's or higher.

You should INVEST some time compiling and reviewing your Opportunity Table to identify the activities and situations in which you SPEND time and WASTE time that keep your Happiness Score under 90. Once you see your data, some of your corrective actions will likely be obvious. Again, refer back to Chapter 18 to help you compile your data in your "Opportunity Table." Write down your corrective actions. Keep the list private and safe to ensure your safety unless you can safely share information with licensed professionals or others who you are sure can help without causing harm. Then take action, monitor your progress and celebrate victories, big and small.

HAPPINESS SCORE 50-75

Many of you have a Happiness Score between 50 and 75 which means that you're in the yellow zone most of the time, except maybe on weekends when you likely have more control of your time.

In the 50-75 range, you are probably not thrilled with your work or not very engaged in your occupation. If so, you probably need to take a hard look at your workplace or your occupation and ask yourself, should I **fix it**, **live with it** or **leave it**? Remember, if you don't **fix it** and you perceive that you can't **leave it**, then that means that you are essentially choosing to **live with it**. That might be the correct decision, especially if safety or basic needs are at risk. If that's the case, make sure that compromise is your true choice on purpose.

Alternatively with a score of 50-75, you might actually be enjoying your occupation, but something else is amiss in your relationships, or your second job or you have a tremendous number of logistical burdens on which you SPEND time.

If this sounds like your situation, you should really compile your Opportunity Table as described in Chapter 18 and analyze in writing exactly where you are SPENDING time, WASTING time and how you will resolve at least the most crucial specific activities and their causes. Keep the list private and safe to ensure your safety, unless you can safely share information with licensed professionals or others who you are sure can help without causing harm. Again, once you have the written list, write down potential solutions to convert SPEND time activities and WASTE time activities into INVEST time or SLEEP. Remember, some SPEND time activities are unavoidable, so don't feel bad if you can't write down a solution for each one.

With a Happiness Score of 50-75, it is also possible that you enjoy your occupation and MOST of your relationships, but you are experiencing harm in WASTE time activities, that may be limited to one or more stressful relationships or circumstances. If safety or risk are potentially threatening your situation, you may need to be creative in ensuring that you safely get the help of licensed professionals, maybe even the police.

As always, keep in mind that if you or someone you know is struggling or in crisis, help is available. In the United States, call or text 988 or chat 988lifeline.org (988 Suicide & Crisis Lifeline).

HAPPINESS SCORE UNDER 50

If your Happiness Score is less than 50 (including negative scores), major changes in your life are likely necessary if you ever want to **BE HAPPIER**. A Happiness Score under 50 is in the red zone and professional intervention may very likely be required (as long as you can get that intervention safely).

With a Happiness Score under 50, you are likely experiencing multiple harmful WASTE time situations. In particular, you may be having major challenges in safety, relationships and at work. A detailed analysis of INVEST time, SPEND time and WASTE time may be insufficient to resolve multiple serious WASTE time situations using simple commonsense solutions. If you can get professional help safely, that is a path you should carefully consider. Remember, safety is paramount. As always, keep in mind that if you or someone you know is struggling or in crisis, help is available. In the United States, call or text 988 or chat 988lifeline.org (988 Suicide & Crisis Lifeline).

Sometimes, when the Happiness Score is under 50, circumstances beyond your control are at work. For example, on February 23, 2022, Ukrainians in Kyiv were socializing with their friends and family in cafés. A day later on February 24, their lives were turned upside down by the Russian attack on their country and within a few months, 12 million Ukrainians out of 44 million were displaced from their homes, of which 5 million left the country. Families were separated. Even though the analysis is always valid that in a difficult situation, you have only the three choices of **fix it, live with it** or **leave it, sometimes circumstances are so difficult beyond a person's control that making lists and simple commonsense solutions are inadequate**. As mentioned earlier, my father endured 3.5 years of slavery in death camps and labor camps and he figured out how to **live with it** without knowing if he would die or be liberated. After the atrocities were over, he proactively lived another 70 years with purpose and fulfillment.

The point is that I do not want to misrepresent or oversimplify. Not all unhappiness in all situations, especially in extreme situations, can be resolved by measuring your Happiness Score, analyzing the components in the Opportunity Table and figuring out simple solutions.

At the same time, I do want to point out that most of us are not subject to the horror of inescapable inhumane circumstances. Most of us **_CAN_** exert a certain amount of control over our lives in societies that are stable enough to reasonably expect "life, liberty and the pursuit of happiness."

HAPPINESS SCORE = 100

If you measured your Happiness Score and the result was 100, then you didn't measure properly or you're lying to yourself. Do you really not pay bills, never had a headache or toothache? Some activities that you don't enjoy are simply unavoidable. That's life.

If you see value in measuring your Happiness Score, go back, remeasure and reanalyze. Your Opportunity Table will help but only if you are honest with yourself enough to record your activities of SPEND time and WASTE time.

WHAT ARE YOU NOW GOING TO DO?

Do you have an absolute obligation to measure your Happiness Score, compile your Opportunity Table and modify your behavior? No.

But it's **YOUR** life.

Only **YOU** know how happy you are. Only **YOU** know how much happier you want to be. Only **YOU** can decide what actions you will take, IF ANY, to improve **YOUR** life, as the **clock keeps ticking independently of your action or inaction**!

I can't imagine that you read this entire book (that you have now almost completed) and you say to yourself "Nah, I'll just continue to do what I always have done!" unless your Happiness Score is above 90. But that's up to **YOU**!

I will probably never meet you or know you personally or find out your Happiness Score. Whatever it takes for you to **BE HAPPIER** is between <u>YOU</u> and <u>YOU</u> (possibly affecting or affected by others around you such as children, life partners and others).

The point is that as author of this book, I am not your accountability partner. All I did was present you with simple tools, which are the Happiness Score, the app "**Be Happier**," the Opportunity Table plus <u>a</u> lot of pages of common sense organized into chapters. That's all! Everything else is totally up to you (assuming you can make changes safely).

So, what are you now actually going to do?

If you agree with the common sense presented in this book, you should consider performing the following steps:

1. Track the activities and time that you INVEST, SPEND, WASTE and SLEEP.

2. Identify **<u>IN WRITING</u>** your opportunities to convert SPEND time and WASTE time into INVEST time or SLEEP. Use the Opportunity Table to make it easier to identify the opportunities. Keep your list private and safe unless you can ensure your safety, sharing it with selected professionals or others who you're sure can help.

3. Put **<u>IN WRITING</u>** potential action steps to **<u>fix it</u>**, **<u>live with it</u>** or **<u>leave it</u>**. Keep these potential action steps even more private and safe unless you can ensure your safety when sharing it with selected professionals or others who you're sure can help and are trustworthy.

4. Decide which action steps you will actually implement, when and in what order.

5. Take action.

6. Monitor your progress.

7. Celebrate victories, large and small.

8. **BE HAPPIER**

WHAT ARE YOU NOW GOING TO DO?

Final Comments

On my 21st birthday, I told my father that I had no future. I was left back in 11th grade and I couldn't get into college. I perceived that I had no useful skills in society since all I learned in the previous three years in the military was how to load and maintain anti-aircraft missiles and launchers in the desert. I was also a social failure and I did not yet have my first girlfriend. **I was depressed most of the time, angry the rest of the time and felt worthless all of the time**.

I am now sitting in an apartment in Venice, Italy writing a book about happiness.

How can this be?

I want people who are not happy to **BE HAPPIER**. I want people who are already happy to **BE HAPPIER**.

Somehow, I made the transition from being angry and depressed with little hope for any part of life to be acceptable, to my reality today which is enjoying 43 years of marriage to one outstanding woman, having two adult children of whom I am very proud (AND their spouses), enjoying my grandchildren more than anything, loving my multiple occupations in breakthrough R&D, passive investing, small business coaching (especially strategic business analysis) and now bringing the simple, objective and compelling Happiness Score and Opportunity Table to people who want or even NEED to **BE HAPPIER**.

Read the previous paragraph again and pay special attention to the order in which I cited the areas that bring me happiness. Relationships are #1. Occupation is #2.

I practice what I preach. Enjoying fulfilling and satisfying **RELATIONSHIPS** has been my #1 source of happiness in my irreversible decades of life that I started to enjoy when I met my wife, a few years after my 21st birthday. Enjoying fulfilling and satisfying

OCCUPATIONS has been my #2 source of happiness in my irreversible decades of life that I started to enjoy a few years after my 21st birthday.

Meanwhile, during my **life journey from hopelessness to happiness**, my scientific mind was unconsciously at work, gathering and analyzing data, until one day, I clearly saw that **my happiness was a direct product of the personal choices I had made.** This revelation eventually led to my formulation of the Happiness Score Equation and the Opportunity Table that I share with you today.

WHY THE BOOK AND THE APP "BE HAPPIER?"

I know what it is like to go from the bottom of the barrel to standing on top of a mountain. I want everyone to experience the joy and happiness that I have.

My goal in writing this book was not to provide multiple mushy inspirational statements of "Yes you CAN do it" or to make a non-comprehensive laundry list of 15 things you can do to **BE HAPPIER** that may or may not be relevant to your situation. My goal was to provide you with very practical and simple tools to analyze your happiness so that you can make whatever transition you choose by deciding which actions to take to customize solutions for <u>**YOUR**</u> life (on the condition that you can do this safely).

It is my sincere hope that your goal will be to utilize this information and these easy-to-use tools to change your life from this moment forward (on the condition that you can do this safely).

The clock is ticking whether you're happy or not.

You might as well **BE HAPPIER** from now and for every moment of the rest of your irreversible life.

It's your choice to **BE HAPPIER**.

Now take action!

NOW BE HAPPIER!

About the Author

Marc Halpern is an international speaker, author and practitioner in the fields of industrial organic chemistry, real estate investing, strategic business analysis, R&D management and self-improvement. Marc applies critical thinking skills and creativity used to achieve chemical technology breakthroughs to investing, business analysis and happiness.

In his lecture "Self-Image Tune-Up: How to Improve Personal Performance," Marc describes a very simple, fun and practical method to reach life goals. Marc is passionate about helping people realize their potential.

In addition to his book, *Now Be Happier*, Marc innovated the concepts of the "Happiness Score" and the "Opportunity Table" as described in this book and his 2022 TEDx lecture. These concepts are also showcased in the "**Be Happier**" app.

Marc currently lives in New Jersey with his wife of 43 years where they enjoy a stress-free marriage and spend quality time with their adult children and grandchildren. Marc achieved all of his major goals for happiness in family life, occupation and self-actualization.

Stay tuned for more Now Be Happier programs and training. You can learn more and see what's new at www.NowBeHappier.com.